Is There
Life After
High School?

Is There Life After High School?

Making Decisions about Your Future

STEVE SWANSON

Augsburg ◆ Minneapolis

IS THERE LIFE AFTER HIGH SCHOOL?
Making Decisions about Your Future

Scripture quotations unless otherwise noted are from the Holy Bible: New International Version. Copyright 1978 by the New York International Bible Society. Used by permission of Zondervan Bible Publishers.

Cover design: Terry Dugan

Library of Congress Cataloging-in-Publication Data

Swanson, Steve, 1932–
    Is there life after high school? : making decisions about your future / Steve Swanson.
      p.   cm.
    Summary: Guides Christian high school graduates on the possibilities of life, career, college, sex, and marriage.
    ISBN 0-8066-2500-7
    1. Vocation—Juvenile literature.   2. Teenagers—Vocational guidance—Juvenile literature. [1. Decision making.
2. Vocational guidance.   3. Christian life.] I. Title.
BV4740.S92   1991
248.8'3—dc20
                                     90-15499
                                        CIP
                                        AC

Manufactured in the U.S.A.   AF 9-2500

95   94   93   92   91   2   3   4   5   6   7   8   9   10

To the world's
wonderful teachers,
yours and mine—
in church, neighborhood,
home, and school—
who help us adventure our way
down life's paths
by sharing with us many
of the values and skills
that we need
to survive.

Contents

1

Is There Life after High School?

*B*ecause you hold this book in your hands, you care—or someone who loves you cares—what you are about to do with the rest of your life.

Lives can be spent, invested, given, squandered, dedicated, frittered away, or endured. Lives can take shape in perhaps a dozen other ways too—some better than others. But life *will be lived.* Some of your life, for better or for worse, is already behind you, but there's a whole lot more of it out there waiting for you. Your challenge is to make the rest of it good, useful, and worthwhile—yes, and even fun.

As a Christian, of course, your life is not entirely your own. God has a stake in how you live your life and what you do with it. Also, as Christians you and I believe that Jesus died for us. He invested *his* life in *your* life. You are a redeemed, saved, bought-and-paid-for person. You are therefore valuable and important. You already mean a lot to Jesus. He wants that fact to make a difference in the rest of your life. That's the Holy Spirit's work.

The Spirit is there for you so that you don't have to make your life decisions alone. The Spirit will be by your side always, helping you decide, steering you (perhaps not always in a perfectly straight line, but always inching you toward what God intends for your life).

This book is designed to help you consider some options and possibilities. It is also intended to offer hope. God has put an exciting world out there for you and for all of us. There's a terrific life out there ahead of you, a wonderful life. There are people to meet and to work with out there. There are people to be friends with and to love—perhaps one to marry. There are opportunities you haven't even dreamed of. It's all just waiting for you.

Many young people today are chained to a sinking ship called despair. They have lost a lot of hope. Some of this despair comes from living in the nuclear age. "If we're all going to blow up anyway," they think, "what does it matter what I do?"

Look at it positively. Nuclear weapons are so horrible and so capable of quick delivery anywhere in the world, that world wars—unless started by accident—now seem out of the question. A terrible world war ended in 1918 and another one—even worse—ended in 1945 with the use of nuclear weapons. Those wars were only about twenty years apart. Although Korea, Vietnam, and the Persian Gulf have had their own horrors, we have gone fifty years without a world war and without nuclear weapons being used on *anybody.* So, in a crazy sort of way, nuclear weapons—as frightening and stupid and expensive as they are—may have saved a future for you that otherwise might not have been.

Sometimes despair also comes from stockpiling a whole lot of unhappiness. Young people can be troubled by many things: the divorce of their parents, abuse by adults, lack of roots, a miserable self-image, losing friends, bad times in school, unwise decisions about sex or drugs.

This book does not address all those problems, but if your teen years have been pretty much a bad scene, better things can come—much better things. God can help you make your future more satisfying than your past.

Sometimes despair comes from having too many choices. There are so many different kinds of jobs out there today that one often doesn't have the faintest notion where to start looking—or to start training. Especially women.

When your grandmother was young, there were only about three accepted professions for her to consider. Women could be teachers, nurses, or housewives. *And* there were only about three jobs. Women could be secretaries, clerks, or salespersons.

Vocational guides now list thousands of jobs and professions for *both* men and women. Women now can be doctors, lawyers, pastors, firewomen, electrical and telephone linewomen, policewomen—you name it.

All of those options might be confusing at first. But really, would you want to go back to Grandma's time? Think of the world of opportunities.

There are wonderful jobs and exciting challenges out there waiting for you. Most didn't *exist* fifty years ago. God knows the opportunities you will face and wants to show you how to take advantage of them—starting today!

So open your mind. Be prepared to try many different things and to fail at some of them. Be prepared to pray a whole lot, and to listen and learn as you go. Sometimes we are guided through the hallways of our lives by having doors shut and even locked in our faces. Sometimes a closed door helps us notice that other doors are open. Some of them are *wide* open. Because God has promised to be with you always, sooner or later God will lead you through the right doors.

I hope this book will help. Read it. Share it with your friends. Talk to your parents, your pastors, your teachers, and your counselors about your hopes and dreams for the future. People like that are often God's agents in disguise, God's wonderful shepherds who are especially programmed to help get you to where you should go.

God has wonderful things in store for your life. God bless you as you explore the opportunities you meet along the way.

Read on.

2

I Am a Many-layered Person

*J*enny sat with Consuela on "Connie's" front step. It was a good time for Jenny to have her best friend beside her. Jenny was confused and slightly frightened; being with Connie helped a lot. The two of them just sat there for a long time and stared into space.

"It's not the end of the world," Connie said at last.

"I know that," Jenny replied, swatting a fly away from her face.

"You'll find out who you are and what you're supposed to do after you've tried a few things."

"It would take forever to try all the things people want me to do. Everyone wants me to try something different. Mom wants me to be a teacher, Grandma wants me to be a missionary, and Scott wants me to hurry up and marry him as soon as possible."

"Scott can wait," Connie said, pointing her finger like a kindergarten teacher. "Just tell him to cool it. You have to go to college first."

"But what college? And to study what? And what if I study one thing all through college and then find out it isn't what I want to do?"

"That wouldn't be the worst. That wouldn't be as bad as, let's see, as . . . having all your hair fall out the night before your wedding."

Jenny laughed and hugged Connie. Laughing helped.

◆

Jenny and Connie were talking about a common teenage problem. Between ages eighteen and twenty-one, most young people are job hunting, or studying and training in order to get a job later, and it always seems serious and it always seems urgent.

Like Jenny, most Christian young people would like to have God whisper in their ears and say, "Jenny, you're an architect," or "Pete, you're a cabinetmaker," or "Connie, you're a computer programmer," or, "Ryan, you're a forest ranger."

But God usually doesn't do that. Only a rare few people hear the voice of God or even feel a distinct call from God. Some of them have interesting stories. Gladys Aylward's story is depicted in the film *The Inn of the Sixth Happiness* (starring Ingrid Bergman). If it ever comes on late night TV, watch it. Better yet, get the book (*The Small Woman*, by Alan Burgess) from your library and read it.

Gladys Aylward was a household servant in England. She felt strongly that God had called her to work in China. She went to a missionary training school, but after three months they told her she wasn't a good student, and because she was over twenty-five, they felt she would have trouble learning the many dialects in the Chinese language.

But it was God's call after all, and flunking out of school didn't stop her. Soon an opportunity came. With little money and not much more than her faith and her calling, she took a boat to Europe and a train through Russia. It was 1930. Russia and China were at war. She was stranded, ordered off trains at gunpoint, robbed, and shot at— but she finally got to China. She worked there for the next dozen years, capping her faithful service by aiding the wounded and saving many orphaned children in the terrifying early years of World War II.

God does not call most of us so distinctly. In my life I have wanted to be (and in some cases have been): a civil engineer (surveyor), a meteorologist (weatherman), a physicist, a skating clown in a professional ice show, an English teacher, a navy chaplain, a writer, a pastor, a commercial fisherman, and a playwright. This is not to mention the many things I have done and continue to enjoy doing that I always knew wouldn't be my profession: carpentry, electrical wiring, auto mechanics, and coaching.

We are many-layered persons, all of us. Even some of the things that don't seem so important right now are often indicators of abilities, skills, talents, and tendencies that could someday lead to a profession or a career.

Just look around you. Wouldn't you think that your pastors and your school counselors were probably good listeners when they were young? Even in junior high or high school, wouldn't they have been the kinds of people whose friends kept confiding in them, the ones who were entrusted with secrets?

And wouldn't you guess that the shop foreman at the car repair shop downtown was already a car nut when he was younger? Wouldn't you expect that your band or choir directors were always rather musical, and that your coaches were always rather athletic?

Now, a chemist or historian can also be musical or sports-minded. I knew a wrestling coach who taught archeology, and a football coach who was the college pastor. One of my good friends teaches high school English, tends twelve acres of Christmas trees, is a ski instructor, and is one of my summer fishing guides.

Jenny hasn't really taken a good inventory of her skills and talents and tendencies yet. You'll watch her do that as you read further in this book. You'll see who she goes to for help, listen to what advice she gets, and notice how some of her earliest leadings and dreams send her in certain directions.

Some of the people she talks to will remind her that the average person has three and four vocations in a lifetime and up to fifteen different jobs. It should be plain that Jenny doesn't have to choose her first job as if it were going to be her only job ever. You don't, either. You will change jobs often, and each job will lead to something else. Each kind of work is a learning experience, even if it seems a miserable mistake.

Jenny will be reminded and will remind herself that as a Christian young person, God wants her to live a life of service. That doesn't mean she *has* to be a missionary or a pastor, although some people serve in those professions.

Jenny can serve God in anything she is led to do. Her friend Connie would probably add, "except maybe being a bank robber."

Service to God has little to do with how you and I earn our living. Look at the people you respect and love around town, around church, and around school. A Christian janitor or cook is just as important as a Christian teacher or superintendent. We serve God where we are and however we spend our days.

So Jenny is off on her quest. She has her mom, her boyfriend Scott, her friend Connie, her pastor, her youth leader at church, the people at school, and a whole lot of others to help her in her search. Although many people are usually involved, in this book we'll focus on her conversation with Ann, her youth leader.

Watch Jenny carefully. Her search may turn out to be something like yours.

3

Does God Have a Special Plan for Me?

*L*ook," Connie said, standing up to adjust her jeans, then sitting. "I can't let you mope around here all year. We're seniors. We're supposed to be having fun."

"It's not much fun yet." Jenny frowned.

"If you could decide some things this month, you could still get applications off to a school or whatever."

"It's too late already," Jenny said.

"No it's not. Besides, maybe you'll decide to work a year before you go to school. Then you'll have more time. Either way, you need to talk to someone right now."

"I've gone to meetings at school. I've seen the counselor. I've even taken tests. It doesn't help." Jenny shrugged and threw up her hands. "God only knows what I should do."

"Maybe *that's* where you should start"—Connie snapped her fingers and pointed—"on the God part."

"You mean try to find out God's plan for my future? Like, what does *God* want me to do with my life?"

"Yeah. Like that."

"How do I find that out?"

"I guess you should go ask some 'God' person. How about your pastor?"

"His wife is having a baby. He's at the hospital."

"Really? You'd never find our priest at the hospital for *that!* So who else is there at your church?"

"The youth leader: Ann. You've met her."

"Yeah, I have. She's nice. Why don't you go talk to her?"

"I don't know." Jenny shook her head slowly.

"Come on, Jenny," Connie said, getting up off the step and pulling at Jenny's arm. "Come on in the house. I'll even call Ann for you, then I'll walk you over to your church."

◆

"So, Jenny, what's up?" Ann asked when Jenny came in.

"I'm up to here, that's what's up," Jenny said, putting all her fingernails against the underside of her jaw. "I've had it with everybody in my class! They all know what they're going to do and where they're going."

"Next year, you mean?"

"Not only next year but for their whole lives, from the way it sounds."

"And the problem is that you *don't* know, right?"

"Right," Jenny said.

"Have you taken any tests at school? Like interest tests or vocational aptitude tests?"

"I took two." She held up two fingers. "They made things even worse. One test said I should be a nurse. What a joke."

"Why?"

"I faint if someone even has a bloody nose! I couldn't stand surgery."

"Not all nurses work in surgery."

"But they have to do that stuff in training. And they have to care for people. Bedpans. Rotting sores. Yuck!" Jenny held her nose. "I wouldn't be able to stand the smells."

"So much for that test. How about the other one?"

"That was even worse. *Be a chef,* it said. I suppose that was because I said I like to cook."

"So what's wrong with that? I think cooking in a big hotel would be exciting—and rewarding too."

"I just like to cook at home, for Mom and me. And I like to try something different every time."

"Wouldn't that be good for a chef?"

"Some of my experiments aren't fit to eat. Besides, I want to do something that helps people."

"Eating helps people," Ann chuckled. "It helps keep them alive."

"You know what I mean."

"Like nursing, but without the blood."

"Yeah. Or something like you do," Jenny said, sweeping her arm to encompass Ann's office.

"You mean my job looks good to you?" Ann asked.

Jenny nodded.

"I never planned on doing this. Sometimes you just fall into certain things. That's what I did."

"How?"

"I worked with a church youth group when I was in college, more or less just for fun. When I graduated they hired me. I just stayed there. The pay was terrible, but it meant I didn't have to job hunt—not even one day—or worry at all. And I've never had to dress up." Jenny and Ann laughed because they were dressed exactly alike: jeans, sweatshirt, and tennis shoes. Ann went on: "I've been working with young people ever since—and I've enjoyed it. This is my third youth director job."

"I wish it was that easy for me. Did you know that was what God wanted you to do?"

"Not at first. I had grander plans. But this has worked out—and I like it. I think that *for now*, this is what God wants me to be doing."

"What do you mean, 'for now'?" Jenny asked.

"I mean there may be something different later on. God may not have just one plan for any of us, or just one place. Sometimes one thing is just to get us started toward another."

"But where am *I* supposed to start?"

"Got any dreams of what you'd like to be?"

"Oh, the usual stuff," Jenny laughed and shrugged her shoulders. "Movie star, rock singer, astronaut, governor, president."

Ann laughed with her. "I know you're kidding—for the most part—but do you know that every one of those dreams has a connection with courses they teach in college: drama, music, astronomy, political science?"

"You don't get to be president by taking a course in political science."

"Maybe not, but it's a place to start. I know a governor who started by organizing a political club in college. So how about other vocations: computers, dentistry, secretarial work, architecture, building trades, engineering? Anything like that?"

"Nothing."

"How are your grades in school?" Ann asked in a confidential tone.

"Only one or two were lower than a B."

"Well you wouldn't get into Vassar or Harvard, but there are plenty of colleges and universities that would take you. Do you like school?"

"Most of the time."

"A liberal arts college is a wonderful place to start if you don't know for sure where you want to end up. They make you try different things. 'Distribution' it's usually called. Sometimes as you take different kinds of courses, you sooner or later run into something you really like."

"What was *your* major in college?" Jenny asked.

"I majored in religion to start with, then my advisor told me I had to take a literature course. The only one open that term was called The Russian Novel. That spring I fell in love with Russia. When I graduated I had majors in religion and Russian literature, and a minor in Russian language.

"You should be a *missionary* to *Russia!*" Jenny shouted.

"I thought we were talking about what *you* should do," Ann laughed.

4

Should I Go to College?

*J*enny and Ann talked about a lot of things, but the idea of college was underneath everything they said. Jenny knew that she would go to college in the next year or two, and Ann assumed that about her as well.

Not everyone is so sure. Even if you are sure, it's just the beginning. *The Random House Dictionary* (Random House, 1987) lists over 2,400 colleges in the U.S. and its territories and over 250 colleges in Canada. The list is many pages long—and in small print—and includes symbols indicating size, degrees offered, and who sponsors or owns each school. Some almanacs and reference books in your school counselor's office will list not only schools, but also the amount of each school's tuition and fees (from under $2,000 to over $20,000 a year). Each school has its own specialties and its own uniqueness. A star football player, for instance, will choose one school, a champion chess player another, and an accomplished musician or actress yet another.

But should Jenny go at all? Should you? And should you start the autumn after you finish high school? And how do you choose just one from among 2,500-plus schools?

There are no easy answers to these questions. Our oldest son graduated from college in 1988. He was thirty-one. He went to one college right out of high school. He successfully completed one year, but then dropped out to work for a few years. He became interested in ceramics and developed skill at the potter's wheel, built kilns, burners, racks, and bought clays and glazes. Then he went for a semester to a second college that had a strong ceramics department. Later he got married and built a pottery studio.

Two years later his pottery shop burned to the ground. That small tragedy provided an opportunity for reassessing his goals. Instead of rebuilding the shop, he went back to college and earned a bachelor's degree. He is working again, and beginning to think about graduate school in ceramics and art.

I suppose we should have worried some that his education took so long. Some parents get mighty upset when their sons and daughters postpone college. Their fears are sometimes founded. Some young people get caught up in other activities and other work and never do go. Some start college, drop out for various reasons, and never go back. (That's not the end of the world.)

Jenny and Ann talked about how a liberal arts college helps a person decide what kind of jobs he or she might like. That also happens in the workplace. Working a year or two after high school, even at McDonald's or the corner gas station, may help you discover that you never want to sell anything again in your whole life—or deal with customers either. You may discover just the opposite. Maybe you'll like commerce and sales and when you do go to school you may lean toward business administration, management, or accounting.

You can learn a lot about the higher levels of certain kinds of work, and how you feel about them, by getting involved in the lowest entry levels of that work. That's true even of summer jobs. If you get a job as a candy striper or an assistant janitor in your local hospital, you will soon develop some attitudes about the work of nurses, doctors, hospital administrators, medical lab technicians, dieticians, and all the rest. Work in a retirement center and you'll learn the same things about those who care for older people.

Stock shelves in a hardware store. Be a mail clerk in a publishing house. Be a waiter or waitress or cook's assistant in a fine restaurant. Be an errand runner in your state legislature. Go on a dig with the state archeological society. Work in a Bible camp or a nursery school. Get on a crew that does landscaping, road construction, cement work, home building, or tree planting. No matter what job you try, you'll learn a lot about yourself. In the process you will also get a clearer view of where you might want to be ten years later, and of how further education might help get you there.

You don't, of course, have to go to college to do well in this life. One of the successful businessmen in my town didn't finish college. Indeed, he didn't even finish high school. He couldn't read or write. He was dyslexic. He still is. Forty years ago no one even *knew* that word.

He still doesn't read or write very well. His wife (and business partner) handles all the correspondence and the books. It's obvious that there's nothing else wrong with his mind, except for the way his brain scrambles up words on paper.

If you are reading these words, you're probably not dyslexic. The chances are you have recently finished high school or have a year or so left to go. Should you go to college? Right after you graduate? Should you stay in college if you're there now?

Yes.

I recommend college as soon as possible and as long as possible for anyone who can do the work. I also urge my advisees and college students toward graduate school. I advise them to take as much higher education as they can handle, afford, or stomach. I spent fourteen years in the classroom after high school. We had three children when I started graduate school and five (one adopted) before I finished. We were at times very poor. Broke. But I've never regretted it. I've never met anyone who regretted spending too much time in school. Most regret not spending *enough* time, or spending too much time studying things they *had* to, rather than subjects they *wanted* to.

So do it. Take all the college work you can handle. The intensity varies a great deal, of course. Your regional state college won't be half as tough as Yale—and will be a whole lot cheaper. Anyone who has no learning disability and who is willing to apply himself or herself can graduate from some college, somewhere, somehow—and can also manage some way to pay for it.

The larger college question for most of you reading this is not *whether*, but *when*. Should I go now or postpone going for a while?

For the last decade our colleges and universities have been filling up with some of the dropouts from the sixties and seventies. Back when these former dropouts were eighteen to twenty, they saw college as the enemy, the Establishment, and wanted no part of it. Now, as thirty- and forty-year-olds, they're back in class. I've taught them. They're wonderful: highly motivated, much more experienced, and deeply intolerant of busy work and irrelevant, hypothetical discussions. They want up-to-date information that they can use and apply right now. Because they have started late, they want to hurry and get on with their lives. The World War II ex-servicemen who went back to college between 1945 and 1950 were much the same way.

You needn't drop out like that, though, nor wait that long. Those who aren't sick of books and classes and studying when they finish high school often go right to college. Such high school graduates take good advantage of the momentum they have going and it usually works out fine. After a summer's rest and work (a summer does wonders for those I-never-want-to-see-another-book feelings), they plunge right into college life and thrive—and love it.

If you aren't sure, though, and if you aren't motivated, and if you really, down deep in your

27

heart, don't want to start college right away, then go ahead and work for a year or two. It won't hurt.

But during that time investigate your college and university options. Get catalogs from your school counselor or the public library, or write to schools that interest you and ask for information. Study their programs, course offerings, and financial aid packages. Make phone calls. Write letters. Dream dreams. The schools of your choice will help you in every way they can.

Many people apply to a number of colleges in the hope that they will be accepted by at least one. You can also apply to a college or university for admission even though you aren't sure you will attend right after high school, maybe not even for a year or two. If they admit you and you don't enroll, just notify the school that you are postponing enrollment and ask them to keep your admission on file. Most schools will do that, even up to several years. Should you decide to go there later, they will often let you start without even reapplying.

Meanwhile, don't lose out on a college education by default. Older students are indeed wonderful, but many say they're sorry they missed out on the teenage side of college life. It's different when you're forty. You may have a husband or wife at home—and children—and you aren't as likely to get involved in the social life of college, the romances (certainly not if you're married!), the athletics, the volunteer activist groups, the dormitory nightlife (the all-night arguments about politics, philosophy, or religion), and of course all-night study sessions.

When you're a lot older it's a lot different.

So postpone college for a year or two at most. Then get at it.

5

But There Are Thousands of Colleges

*A*nn opened an almanac and showed Jenny a list of hundreds and hundreds of North American colleges and universities. Jenny asked sadly, "How am I going to choose?"

"It's hard," Ann said, "but not as hard as you'd think from looking at that list. Start your selection process with some geography and sociology and history and religion—and then add some hopes and dreams."

"How does that work?"

"Start with geography. When you go to college, how far from home do you want to be?"

"I don't know," Jenny said, thinking for a minute. "I guess far enough so I wouldn't go home every time I had the sniffles, but not so far that I couldn't get home for Thanksgiving and a few weekends."

"That's the way most people figure," Ann said, "kind of a regional choice. From 50 to 250 miles."

Ann got up and walked to the photocopier in her office and began to make copies of pages from the open almanac. "When you get home, take this list and get out a map and a compass or a string with a pencil tied to it. Then draw circles around your home at the 50-, 100-, and 250-mile marks."

"That'll still be a lot of schools."

"I know. That's why we go next to sociology. What schools have your friends gone to? How do they like them? Is there anyone in your high school you'd really like to share a college with?"

"I can think of a few. Like Connie." Jenny smiled just thinking of her.

"OK. Then history. Your history and your family's history. Did members of your family go to college? Where? Did they like it?" Ann was talking fast, ticking the questions off on her fingers. "Then you. How have you done in high school? Are there some colleges that probably wouldn't accept you because of your grades? And how about paying for it? Are there schools that you absolutely couldn't afford? Are your grades good enough and your family's income low enough so you'd get quite a bit of financial aid?"

"How can *anybody* answer all those questions?"

"Chances are, nobody could—alone. But when you narrow the list to five or six schools, those schools will help you."

"How do I narrow it even that far?"

"That's where hopes and dreams—and religion—enter in. If you wanted to be a research biologist or a foot doctor or a paleontologist, you'd narrow your search easily."

"But I don't *know* what I want."

"What you want then is liberal arts. A college or a university."

"What's the difference?"

"Universities are usually bigger, and also grant master's degrees and doctorates," Ann said. "I talked to Mike Taylor last week. He's at the U. One of his classes has five hundred students. Some of them watch the lecture on closed-circuit TV."

I wouldn't like that." Jenny frowned.

"Mike doesn't mind. He says the lectures are great. He wants to be a chemist, and the U has one of the best chemistry departments in the country."

"I'd rather go to a small college," Jenny said.

"How small?"

"Small enough so I could meet a lot of people."

"I know what you mean. When I was a freshman I knew about half my classmates. And all of my classes were taught by experienced professors."

"Is that unusual?" Jenny asked.

"At universities a lot of teaching is done by teaching assistants. Graduate students."

"Students teaching students?"

"Uh huh. Most of the important professors only lecture and do research. A lot of them don't really teach at all."

"Small college for me."

"Fine. That narrows your choices considerably. Then there's religion. Do you want to go to a church college?"

"My mom would want me to."

"Would you?"

"I guess I wouldn't mind."

"There are sometimes disadvantages. Members of smaller denominations may have to travel many miles to go to one of their own colleges. Some religious schools are a bit narrow and over-protective. But mostly they offer a good education with a plus."

"What's the plus?"

"Christian students and professors. People who care about each other."

"I'd like that, I think."

"It's nice," Ann said. "When I went to Brenton, several times different professors took me aside. One told me if I wanted to keep my grades up I had better cut back on extracurricular things."

"Sounds like my mother." Jenny snorted.

Ann laughed. "Another one warned me about a guy I was dating."

"Really?"

"Sure. He was right, too. I was a freshman. Didn't know *anything*. That guy turned out to be a real jerk."

"Wow," Jenny said. "Teachers like that would make it easier, less scary."

Ann nodded. "There are teachers like that everywhere, not just in church colleges. You find them when you look. It's just that the percentage tends to be higher in church colleges. However, having professors who care doesn't make the work any easier. The best church colleges are just as competitive as any other private college."

"So it gets scary again."

"Sometimes, but there are ways to make the academics less frightening. If you are willing to spend an extra semester or year, you can take a reduced load at the beginning."

"Fewer courses?" Jenny sat up straight.

"Yes. And then there are junior colleges. Most of them are good at easing students into college work. They specialize in bringing you up to speed in your weaknesses—let's say, for example, writing, math, and history."

"That might be OK too."

"My younger brother John did that. He and high school didn't get along very well. It offered little to appeal to the developing artistic and visual side of his life. He was always one to work at his own speed—and often at his own projects. He didn't like classroom structure very much.

"In his senior year one of the high school counselors took an interest in him and gave him several tests. She called our mom and said, 'Your John is getting very poor grades.'

'I know,' Mom said.

'But we've just tested him. He's very smart.'

'I know that too,' Mom said.'"

"So what did he do?" Jenny asked.

"That's when Dad got him started at a junior college. He did well and transferred after just one year," Ann went on. "He became an honor student."

"What made him turn around like that?"

"Lots of things, I suppose. His high school counselor. A handful of wonderful teachers at both colleges, different teaching and learning structures, more courses to choose from, motivation. Who knows?"

"Did he change a lot?" Jenny asked.

"Only in some ways. He was still plenty laid back. After four years, even with transferring, he was just two courses short. He decided to take another full semester, a 'fun' semester he called

33

it. He took just the courses he wanted. Along about December he went into the registrar's office to arrange for his graduation the following spring.

'You already graduated,' the registrar said.

'What?'

'Last spring. You were only two courses short. That still qualified you to graduate. Here, look.'

"The registrar pulled out a beautifully engraved folder from the graduation exercises the previous spring. There near the beginning of the list was his name."

"So your crazy brother missed his own graduation!" Jenny laughed.

Ann wasn't exactly laughing when she said, "So did we."

6

What Should I Study?

*T*he basic mental preparation for living and working on this planet hasn't changed much since I was a student. I am a graduate of the school at which I now teach. Even though enrollment has almost doubled and there are more faculty, the only departments that are now listed that I don't remember being there before are dance, Russian and Chinese languages, computer science, and the paracollege (a design-it-yourself style of education).

Liberal arts education hasn't changed much. A few departments have new names—home economics is now called family resources, for instance—and all departments have broadened their scope over the years, but chemistry, classics, economics, political science, religion, and all the other studies I remember are still taught. I don't know of any department that has been dropped. Many departments go back to the founding of the college over one hundred years ago.

That's what makes liberal arts colleges seem old-fashioned. For graduation they require about the same things now as they did back in my time. They ask a student to study English and history and laboratory science and social science and fine arts and physical education and so on. Such colleges say they train the whole person, that their graduates can learn to do almost any job. It's mostly true.

Many people who go to universities specialize. They start out to be electrical engineers and everything they study prepares them specifically for that. There's nothing wrong with that. Even a liberal arts college sooner or later requires some specialization—a major or concentration. That is the cause of much sophomore bewilderment and anguish. "I need to choose a major pretty soon," they moan.

All of them eventually choose. A few have trouble deciding and end up with double or even triple majors. Quite a few have to choose more than once. They change majors.

I did. I had wonderful physics and chemistry teachers both in high school and in my first year in college. I am naturally mechanical and for two years I did well and thought for sure I was a physics major. Then suddenly physics became less mechanical and more electronic—and its problems required more and more calculus. I floundered.

In the middle of my junior year I sat down and asked myself what else I was good at. I came up with athletics and writing. I had already gotten a few A's and B's in the English department. I talked to the chairman. "Sure," he said, and took me in.

That became my new major and my life's work. I have taught literature and writing ever since— and have written books and plays and poems and have had a marvelous time doing it.

That same year I changed positions on the football team as well. I became a lineman, learned how to play that position, and was named all-conference in my senior year. Strangely enough, I also dropped hockey that year. I had been captain in my junior year. As a senior, I decided I'd rather sing in a choir. I was changing. A lot. College was doing things to me.

I met my wife that year too. She was and still is an artist. That got me interested in art. From math and physics and athletics to music and art and literature. College. It did things to me.

The next few years will do things to you as well. God is already nudging you in several directions. You too have gifts. You may already have discovered in yourself people skills or scientific skills or business or artistic or literary or musical or dramatic skills. College will be a time to sort them out. You may not be sure at first which are the most important or which will lead to lifetime interests or careers. It won't matter. Pursue as many as you can, as seriously as you can, and for as long as you can.

There are two ways to go at this sorting and pursuing when you start college and God only knows which will work best for you.

One, *you can go with your strengths*, or, two, *you can go with your dreams*.

Some people have strengths and dreams that are much the same. These are the ones that annoy undecided people like Jenny—the ones who always knew they wanted to be businesswomen or pilots or doctors or opera singers or auto mechanics.

If choosing is not all that easy for you, then in college it might be sensible to start with your strengths and dabble in your dreams. Most people who attend a liberal arts college will find their particular strengths listed among the school's distribution requirements—courses that students have to take sooner or later anyway: music, science, math, history, literature, physical education.

So why not register right away for a course or two in your strength? You'll get good grades, tick off some of your graduation requirements, be farther along on your quest for a major, and maybe, without knowing it, you'll be exploring one of your future career choices. (The average number of lifetime career changes today is three. *Three!*)

But don't forget your dream. Do you dream of a career in singing? Register for voice lessons. Do you want to be an actor or actress? Go out for a play or register for a theater course. Do you want to be an artist? Try drawing, sculpture, ceramics. Do you want to run for governor? Join political clubs. Take a course in political science.

"But what if I fail?" you may ask.

You don't usually fail in college courses if you do your best—you just get lower grades in those you aren't so good at. I have two D's on my college transcript. When I first went in to talk to my advisor and writing tutor in graduate school I was worried about that. He looked at my transcript and mumbled,"You did poorly in just the right things."

We can't all be good at everything. Doing poorly sometimes forces us to change our thinking and redirect our lives. Gail Sheehy in her book *Passages* called college years the "pulling up roots" period and says that although we don't know exactly what we *want* to do, we begin by learning what we *don't* want to do (Bantam, 1977).

You'll never in the many years ahead of you have a better chance to experiment with what you may be good at or enjoy or want to try. Registering for college courses is like Sunday brunch at The Chef. There are so many good things, it's hard to choose. Registration day is a frustrating, wonderful, exciting time.

I'm making it sound like you can try anything you want. Your first year registration day probably won't be that way. You always get *some* of what you want, but the class sections you want the most will often fill up before you even get a chance to register. Tears, anger, and frustration result. Don't be too discouraged if you don't seem to get much choice in your first year or two of college. Tell yourself that these are your years to take care of a lot of your graduation requirements.

Taking introductory courses in history and philosophy and religion will not be a waste of time. Courses like that will help ready your mind for the things you study later. Don't be closed-minded either. Many a student is surprised to discover, as Ann did, that a course taken as a graduation requirement becomes a love, an excitement, even a major. Then the fun begins.

Either way, by the middle of your sophomore year you should be choosing and experimenting freely among departments and courses.

If your grade point average is a serious concern at that time and you still want to try a course that seems like a crazy risk, then take it "pass-fail."

But when you take a course pass-fail, work hard at it anyway.

I've had far too many students register for a writing course pass-fail and then give it only about half a shot. They think, *All I have to do is pass,* so they work at half speed. I always want all my students to give it their best. I always hope some of them may become writers or editors.

For you, too, I hope that experimenting in college will open up a whole new world with new and bigger dreams and often a different and better future from anything you could have dreamed of before.

So search out your strengths—and dreams.

Then go for it.

7

Kissing High School Good-bye

*C*ollege sounds exciting," Jenny said. Just thinking about it made her squirm in her chair.

"It is. And challenging too," Ann said, smiling at Jenny's nervousness.

"But I'll be scared."

"We all are, to begin with."

"High school is so comfortable sometimes."

"I suppose it is. It's so long ago I've kind of forgotten. What's comfortable about it?"

"I know I can make it, for one thing. I get decent grades without really killing myself."

"Did you know that your first year?"

"I suppose not," Jenny said. "I guess I was pretty scared when I moved up from middle school."

"Life is like that. When you go to college you ask, 'Can I make it?' When you go into the Marines and face boot camp you ask, 'Can I make it?' When you go to vocational school or get a job or even bum around Europe for a few months you ask yourself, 'Can I make it?' "

"And what's the answer?" Jenny asked.

"For some it's no. No, they can't make it. They get hung up on drugs or sex or they simply goof off and fail. For you, though, it's yes."

"How do you know?"

Ann began to hum an old fifties tune that was being revived on the radio. Jenny recognized it right away. " 'Via con Dios'!"

"Right. You'll make it because you 'go with God.' But it won't always be easy. What else about high school will be hard to leave behind?"

"My friends, I guess," Jenny said.

"That *is* hard. That's why I asked you before if you might want to go to college with a group of friends."

"That would make it easier."

"You'll do OK, though," Ann said. "You make friends easily. Even for people who don't, it isn't that bad. College or a job or the military are all friend-making situations. You are put next to new people every day. You have roommates, house-mates, barracks-mates. You *have* to relate. Some of them will become friends."

"I suppose so." Jenny nodded.

"What else will be hard to leave?"

"I don't know. I guess getting my school free."

"I know. That was hard for me, too. It's never been free, though," Ann said. "Not really. It's just that in public school all the taxpayers agree to help you."

"I wish they'd keep on!" Jenny said.

"They will, partly. There are government loans. There are scholarships. You can work. You can make it. I guarantee it."

The firmness, the assurance, in Ann's voice made Jenny feel better—but she wasn't completely sure. After a pause she said, "I'm not sure I want to work that hard—or that I can."

"You can—and you will," Ann said. "Everything worth doing in this life is hard work: college, marriage, career, raising kids. Everything. The difference in college is that no one forces you to do it."

"I feel forced in high school. I'm never sure how to feel about the pressure. My teachers are forcing me to produce—expecting it."

"They will expect results in college too. But no one will force you to do anything. No one but you yourself. You'll have a lot more freedom. That sense of Gestapo in high school will be gone."

"What do you mean, Gestapo?"

"Oh, like teachers on patrol in the lunch room and having to get passes to get into and out of class. You're free in college. If you need to get out of class early, many professors won't even expect you to ask. It's polite to *tell* the professor, but he or she probably won't even ask questions. 'Sure,' she'll say. 'Just leave when you have to.' "

"That will really be nice," Jenny said.

"But some kids abuse that freedom. They cut class too much. They let assignments slide. They miss concerts and public lectures that professors assign or suggest. They lose out because all that freedom goes to their heads."

"I hope I won't do that," Jenny said.

"I remember a professor who went to the black-board and figured out for us what each class hour cost. That helped."

"How much *did* it cost?"

"It costs more now than it did. We'll use today's costs. You start with tuition. At a good private school that may be $15,000 a year."

"Wow."

"But that's not all. Add several thousand dollars in book and incidental expenses. Then don't forget that while you're in college you don't work, so that's at least $10,000, probably more, a year you're *not* earning."

"So what's the total?"

"We're already up to $25,000–30,000 a year. You take nine or ten courses a year in most colleges. That's roughly $3000 per course. A course meets eighteen weeks or so, three times a week. What's eighteen times three?"

"Same as nine times six," Jenny smiled.

"Right. Why didn't I think of that? Fifty-four. Round that to fifty. Fifty hours cost $3000. How much is that per hour?"

"Sixty dollars."

"Your college experience is a lot more than just what you learn in class, but when you figure the cost by the class hour, it's not cheap."

"I guess I'll go to every class," Jenny said.

"Well *most* classes anyway. You'll see. You'll want to go most of the time. Professors make you want to. They become friends."

"Friends? Really?"

"Sure. They have an easier time than the teachers you have now. They're not into discipline and control. They don't have to be. They leave that to

44

you—and to the dean of students. That leaves them more time to be partners with you in learning."

"I wish high schools were more like that," Jenny sighed.

"So does everyone. Especially high school teachers."

8

Leaving Home

*L*eaving home can be painful. The pain can be huge or it can be small, it can be short-lived or it can be long-term and nagging. Long or short, large or small, pain is a possibility when you leave home.

Leaving home after high school is the culmination of a process that began when we were born. Inside our mother's womb, we have barely space enough to kick. We are born, put in a basket, then in a crib, then in a bed in a room of our own or with siblings. We start out inside our mothers but once we get out, we move farther and farther away.

Most of you reading this are preparing for the big leap. You've been through moves from womb to crib to bed to a room down the hall. You are now about to put fifty or one hundred or five hundred miles between your family and yourself. In the next five years you may do foreign study, travel, work, or military service that will put you halfway around the *world* from your family.

Beware. As you see this break looming ahead of you, your mind may try to handle that painful experience by beginning to see home as an awful place—a place you *want* to get away from. Once that starts, you will begin to see home as a place where you are overcontrolled, overworked, or overwatched—a place where you are entrapped and smothered. You may overdramatize the situation. If you've ever run away from home temporarily, or if one of your friends has, those were probably the feelings that led up to it.

You don't need to cultivate these feelings to make the break. A major blowup or family war is not necessary to get you out of the family nest. An honest look at your feelings and then some honest talk with parents and siblings should do just as well. Something like this:

MOM: So you're really going to take that job?
SIS: I really am.
MOM: And you're going to live in the big city?
JR.: Can I have her room? Can I?
MOM: Quiet. She hasn't left yet.
SIS: A part of me doesn't want to go.
MOM: I know. Are you scared?
SIS: I'm scared to death.

And so on. Being honest with your feelings and speaking them out loud usually gets a thoughtful, reasonable response. "Response in kind" we call it. But lashing out usually gets a response in kind as well:

SIS: I'm sick to death of this place. I'm glad I'm leaving. All you do is nag.

MOM: I never knew it was SO terrible.

SIS: Well it is.

JR.: I don't think so.

SIS: Shut up, Stupid.

MOM: (*Crying.*) I've tried. Heaven knows I've tried.

SIS: Well I'm trying someplace else.

Prayer is a useful way to prepare for an exchange like this. If you are breaking some big news to your family ("I'm joining the Marines," "I've got this job offer," etc.), then ask God to help *you* in the way you present it, and to help *them* in the way they receive it.

Most parents will try to understand. Most parents will help nudge you gently out of the nest. They know it has to happen. If you feel your mom or someone else in your family clings to you too much, and that your leaving is going to create a big hassle, then get some outside help. Go to your pastor or to a school counselor and talk about this problem and how it might be approached.

God wants to help you become a strong, capable, self-sufficient, and useful person. Getting there is harder for some than for others. God knows that. There is help for you. The power of God is there for you during your breaking away. So are your church and your friends and those adults who have become your confidants and supporters.

Do it without a family war. Wars ta
time to get over. After a war, home may
so much like home anymore.

No matter how far away you go, no ma
long you stay, it's nice to know you alwa
a place to come home to.

If you ask God's help and then move bot
determination and with care, home for yc
be a place where, when you *want* to go
they'll *want* to take you in.

9

Living in Someone Else's Space

*W*hen you leave home," Ann said to Jenny, pointing over the horizon with her pen, "you have to learn to live with some strange people."

"How do you mean?"

"College roommates, for instance. The first year they usually assign you. You could be sharing a room with the daughter of Dracula."

"Don't they even try to find someone you might like?"

"They sometimes have you fill out a questionnaire. They did at Brenton, where I went."

"What do they ask?"

"Oh, like if you're a morning person or a night person. Or whether you'd object to a roommate who smokes. Things like that."

"Does it work?"

"Most of us wondered if they even looked at the questionnaires. I suppose filling them out at least made our mothers feel better."

"What was your roommate like?"

"We were different. We really were. She was big city. Sophisticated. Money in the family. Thought she knew everything about everything."

"So how did it work out?"

"It was awful at first—and I thought it would stay that way. We started to get along after a while, though. We learned from each other, I think."

"Did you room together after that?"

"No. But we stayed friends. We still send each other a note at Christmas."

"Could be worse."

"It is, sometimes. For a lot of kids, college is the first time they have to share anything with anybody, and the first time they haven't gotten their own way about almost everything."

"I'd probably get stuck with someone like that."

"It happens," Ann said. "Sharing comes as a big shock to some people. That's why roommate problems can be so horrible. Fights. Lockouts. Cold wars. And that, of course, leads to informal changes. Roommate swaps. Sleeping on some-one's couch for the last several weeks of a term because you can't stand to be in your own room, things like that."

"Sounds awful."

"It can make studying pretty hard, and college pretty miserable," Ann said. Then after a pause, "Don't worry about it, though. Most of the time it works out OK. And I know it won't be a problem for you. Anyway, after the first year, no one assigns roommates anymore. You start meeting people and ask one of your new friends to room with you—or they ask you! It's hard on the loners—

51

the shy and quiet ones—suddenly they don't have anyone special to room with."

"What then?"

"Either they get brave finally, and ask around, or they get single rooms, or they go to the dean or the housing office to get help. It's worse than that after you graduate."

"What *could* be worse?" Jenny realized her questions were beginning to sound like a broken record. She was learning things though, and didn't want Ann to stop.

"It can be worse when you get a job or go to graduate school in a strange town or city. Sometimes you have to find housing in a place where you know absolutely no one. If there aren't any single units available, or they are way too expensive, you're in trouble."

"Shouldn't you just try to find someone to room with?"

"Sure, but that's not so easy. You can't just put an ad in the paper: 'Pretty girl, alone in the big city, wants a roommate.'"

"That wouldn't be good," Jenny smiled.

"People do advertise for roommates—discreetly. In my second job I started out reading the want ads, but ended up back in church."

"Church?" Broken record again.

"The church that had given me the job. I asked around. A congregation can be helpful in a new situation. Your home pastor may know someone you can contact in the city. He may have the name of the campus pastor at the university. Or you can simply drop in at a neighborhood church and ask for contacts and references. A friend of mine moved into the home of an older couple that way. They treated her like a daughter."

"I wouldn't mind that," Jenny said. "But things are never that easy for me."

"Sometimes you just have to tough it out and start following up the ads you find on bulletin boards or in the paper. Then you're left to trusting your instincts."

"Have you done that?"

"Sure. And it usually works out. It's not like being married. I mean, you don't make vows either to a roommate or to a landlord. You don't *have* to stay. You can move out. Just beware of getting locked into a long-term lease right away."

◆

Ann and Jenny chatted for a while longer about housing and Ann's experiences. They talked about how young people had to live in dormitories and barracks, apartments, in rooms with other families, or live at home and work or go to school.

Barracks, they agreed, have both rules and schedules. Dormitories have only rules. "Living in a dormitory," Ann said, "is like living with one hundred people who all have different schedules and who have dedicated themselves to keeping you awake at all hours. Although everyone seems to *sleep* and *study* at different times, in the morning, strangely enough, they all seem to want to shower and use the toilets *at exactly the same time.* Lunchtime is even worse. So in college you learn to stand in line. You also learn either to become social and enjoy yourself while you stand in line, or else to take work along and read while you stand there."

The phone rang just then. Ann answered and become involved in a conversation. While she waited, Jenny tried to picture herself in a variety of living situations. She thought of herself renting a room in someone else's house. What would it be like? Connie said that her dad, for instance, was always running around in his underwear and shouting at the top of his lungs when he couldn't find a pair of socks or his briefcase.

Jenny pictured herself living in a dorm. What sort of roommate would she be? Could she co-operate? Could she compromise? Could she share? Could she live with someone very different from herself? These were scary questions, but she knew she'd have to face them soon.

Jenny was glad there was no college in town. She tried to imagine herself living at home and going to college. Would her mom still want her to keep a curfew? Would she have to start doing her own laundry? And how about kids who live at home and work? Do they pay room and board or what?

Ann hung up the phone and turned to Jenny, smiling. "Sorry that took so long," she said. "Are you still thinking about dormitories?"

"I am. There are some problems ahead."

"It's like a marriage in one way, though," Ann said. "Most problems in living arrangements can be talked about and discussed. Situations can improve. And of course mutual decisions are usually better than unilateral ones."

"What do you mean?"

"I mean," Ann went on, "for instance, let's say you and someone else share an apartment. As time goes on you both realize that your living together isn't working, but no one talks about that. Both of you like the apartment but because you're not talking about it, both of you go off to other friends and start looking for another place to live. It's a waste of time for one of you."

"You mean that if we *both* find other places to live, then maybe *no one* ends up in the apartment."

"Right. If you and your roommate had been talking to each other about it, even *arguing* with each other about it, at least you might have flipped a coin to see which one would move out. Maybe agreeing on that would lead to agreeing on some other things as well. Maybe then you could part as friends, or at least not as enemies, and not in silence—maybe."

10

Handling Money

*P*roblems in sharing space can often be traced back to attitudes toward money. Sharing an apartment means having to agree on paying your portion of the bills: rent, utilities, phone.

"Who made this call to Spokane?"

"Not me."

"Not me."

There are phantoms in shared apartments who make mystery phone calls to strange places, who eat up other people's food, who wear other people's clothes, and who mislay overdue bills.

Learning to make good decisions about money when you are young will get you off on a lifetime of good credit ratings and a reputation for trustworthy dealings. Bad decisions will do the opposite.

Money decisions, like all decisions, have connections with our faith. After all, money is a major theme in the teachings of Jesus.

A young couple once came to our house and looked at a car I had for sale. After they had test driven it, they told me they had to go home and "pray about it." They must have gotten some sort of answer because they came back the next day and bought the car. They were young and just married so I arranged for them to pay in several installments.

About a year later they tried to resell the car and skin me out of the final payment. I wonder if they also prayed about that, and if so, to whom were they praying?

If our faith doesn't reach way out to where we handle our money, if Jesus isn't somehow involved in how financially honest we are, then what sense does it make?

One of the problems many young people face when they leave home is going instantly from free ride to pay-as-you-go. That's a shock. All the little things they used to take for granted at home suddenly cost a lot of money: shampoo, soap, toilet paper, food, gas, oil changes, insurance, electricity, and RENT. Ouch!

The easy answer for too many new consumers is the little plastic card: credit consumerism. It's an American epidemic. The abuses are unbelievable. I read an article about a man who spent four years juggling about $300,000 in debts among eighteen to twenty credit card companies. One day his card castle tumbled. He declared bankruptcy. It didn't bother him much. For four years he had lived high and lived free on other people's money.

Who then paid the $300,000? Did they make him pay it back? Did the credit card companies pay? The banks? The stores and businesses that had extended him credit?

Of course not. You and I pay that bill. I resent that. I really do. I blame that man's crooked greed and I blame companies who base their business on extending credit to such persons.

I heard the other day that it costs each of us an extra $1000 a year for goods and services to pay bills for companies that extend credit unreasonably and for those jerks who later refuse to pay back those bad debts.

Jesus would not approve.

I don't either.

Suppose you do decide to live on credit. Even if you pay back every penny of what you borrow on consumer credit, even if you never cheat anyone out of a single penny by credit card deferred payments, you are still making a bad decision. You are cheating yourself.

Everything you buy on time payments costs an extra 18-20% a year in interest. In round numbers that means that a $100 item purchased over three years will cost an extra $18 the first year, an extra $12 the second year, and an extra $6 the third year. Three years later your $100 item has cost $136.

Now if you had saved the money up front, if you had waited until you had the cash, the bank would have paid you a few dollars in interest on the money while you were saving it, and if you had walked into the store to buy that $100 item with cash, you could have made an offer and probably gotten a cash discount of 10-15%. The $100 item would then have cost you only $85 cash. Add the $36 interest you would have paid to the

$15 discount you got for cash, and you have saved over half the original cost of the item—*if* you pay cash for it.

So why use credit? Why *ever* use credit? On small items credit makes no sense at all. You may someday have to borrow to buy a house, maybe even your first car, but by the time you are buying your third house and your second car, you should be paying cash. We have bought three houses for cash. We bought only our first car on time payments. That was 35 years and about 150 cars ago. If I had it to do over, I wouldn't even have bought our first car that way. I would have kept driving the old junker I had and saved for something better.

Save first, then buy. Let banks pay *you* interest, not the other way around.

Well, you may think, I won't be able to live on what I earn. You won't if you don't curb your spending, but what sense does it make to borrow or buy on credit to cover the overlap? If you can't live on what you earn, does living on borrowed money and paying an *extra* 18-20% more make any sense?

One of the ways to start thinking right about money is to give some away. We have always given something near a tithe (10%) to the church and to other charities. Starting with 10% less makes you think harder about how to handle the 90% you have left.

A second important decision would be to save an additional 10%. Give away 10% and save 10%. That means living on 80% of your income. If you were to start that pattern now, you'd have money to spare years from now. You'd have a down payment on a house. You'd have cash to pay for your car (and save the one third of the car's price that most people pay in interest on car payments), you'd be lending your kids money to go to graduate school, or buy *their* houses, or start businesses.

Of course, if you do the opposite, if you spend 120% of your income, you'll be dodging bill collectors and bankruptcy for the rest of your life. And, you'll have some terrible fights with your spouse over money.

Credit buying is often a quest for more and more stuff. Look where our consumer, throwaway society has gotten us. We are running out of spaces to bury our garbage.

Learn to live on less. Learn to live on little. Use. Reuse. Recycle. Make do. What do we need with all the junk?

For example, the latest thing in exercise gadgetry is the stair-climbing machine. It can cost up to $2000. A newscaster asked an exercise therapist how using the machine compared to climbing ordinary stairs. "Just about the same," he said.

How far would you have to go to find a flight of stairs to walk up and down? Why then do we need $2000 machines when we all have stairs nearby? How many starving kids somewhere in the world could be fed with that $2000? Where are our priorities?

Another example: one of the newer accessories on an automobile is an instant defrosting windshield. An electric current runs through the whole surface of the windshield and melts off all ice in 20 seconds. If you live in the Midwest—where I do—that sounds pretty nice. But it costs $800 extra. And as long as you own the car, you will pay extra to insure that $800 windshield in case a rock hits it.

Why not get up five minutes earlier and use a scraper? Why not?

This kind of consumer foolishness pervades American society. Middle-class young people have come to think they want, need, or deserve this kind of stuff.

I am constantly appalled when I ask my freshman classes to write an essay on goals and aspirations and most of them say they want good-paying professions, lovely houses, beautiful spouses, expensive cars, and maybe a cabin and a boat thrown in.

These false values often change as students are challenged through their college years, but too many of our young people are grossly materialistic.

God doesn't want to have to dig for you under a pile of consumer junk. God wants your value system to be built on helping, serving, and caring, not on buying, acquiring, and collecting. Wise decisions about money will help steer you away from the one and toward the other.

11

Old Friends and New

*W*hen we stop to think about who Jesus really was and is, we often go back to what churches have taught us. There are two central truths about Jesus: (1) he was and is true God (because he was begotten by the heavenly God), and (2) he was also truly human (because he was born of a human woman, Mary of Nazareth).

Some people find it easy to believe Jesus was and is God. A supreme God is easy to believe in because such a God is so different from what we are.

Some of those same people have a harder time believing Jesus was human, which is to say he was much the *same* as us. Why would God bother? What's so great about being human? we ask.

One thing that makes it easier for me to believe in Jesus' humanness is that he had special friends. But the odd part about his being both human and divine is that as God, Jesus *loves* everyone *equally.* As crazy and difficult as it might seem to us, Jesus loves the guy who has raped and murdered ten children just as much as he loves your dear old saint of a granny.

As a human being, however, Jesus *liked* some people a whole lot better than others. He probably liked Andrew more than Judas, he certainly liked Matthew the tax collector more than Caiaphas the high priest.

Even among his dozen disciples, Jesus had special friends. We call them the "inner circle." Jesus took those three inner-circle friends on his most special ventures: his transfiguration, and the raising from the dead of both Jairus's daughter and Lazarus.

Lazarus was one of Jesus' special friends—and so were Lazarus's sisters Mary and Martha. Because Jesus had those close friends, we can believe he had those same warm and very human feelings that we all have for our best friends.

I think one of the reasons Jesus raised Lazarus from the dead is that he didn't want to experience the painful loss of a best friend through death. If you have lost a friend through illness, accident, or suicide, you know exactly what I mean. You *know* what Jesus felt like as he stood and wept at the door of Lazarus's tomb.

Chaim Potok's superb book, *The Chosen,* is all about friendship and family. One of the fathers in the story quotes from the Talmud, a Jewish holy book of laws and customs. The father says to his son: " 'The Talmud says that a person should do two things for himself. One is to acquire a teacher. Do you remember the other?' 'Choose a friend,' I said."

You have lived long enough to have chosen lots of friends. Some choices were good, some weren't. Some friends have lasted your lifetime so far; some have come and gone. Some have been great; on some you have gotten burned.

Friendship suddenly becomes a hot concern when you are ready to leave home. One of the scary things about leaving your home, your neighborhood, and your high school, is that you also leave behind your friends.

That cozy community where you knew others and they knew you suddenly disappears. Those phone numbers you have had in your head for years will be useless when you leave home because the friends on the other ends of those phone numbers will be leaving too. Sure, you can ring friend Mike's number when you have just gotten a D on your first college math exam, but you'll probably have to be satisfied to talk with Mike's mom or his little sister.

So what do you do?

You make *new* friends.

We never outgrow the selfish habit of choosing friends from whom we want something. We choose friends to help us in business, to help us climb the social ladder, to counsel and console us, to assist us with their skills and abilities, and to make us feel better about ourselves.

But real friendships are not based only on what we can get; they also thrive on what we give. President Kennedy coined the expression: "Ask not what your country can do for you, but what you can do for your country." We could form an equally good motto by substituting the word *friends* for *country*.

During your first days and weeks in a new situation, you will often feel a desperate need to find or to create "community," a place where you can feel at home. You will want friends. We all do, and we want them most desperately when we have none. It's *especially* difficult when everyone else around us seems to have plenty of friends and we don't.

Were you ever the new kid in school? Our daughter Shelley is happily married now and has had troops of friends over the years, but it still breaks my heart to recall how, because she hadn't made any friends in her new school yet, she ate her sack lunches for the whole first week, not in the cafeteria with everyone else, but in the girls' rest room.

Friendship sometimes means reaching out. That's one of the ways Jesus describes the blessed: "I was a stranger and you welcomed me."

Wouldn't Shelley have appreciated—and wouldn't she have considered making friends with—that blessed someone who would have said, "Why don't you come and have lunch with me?"

Maybe instead of worrying about how badly *we* need friends in a new environment, we should look around and try to spot someone who needs a friend even worse than *we* do, then reach out to *that* person.

Those of you who go on to college or to some other kind of training school—or into the military service—will have boundless opportunities to make friends. The whole situation will seem specifically designed to help you meet people. There will be people your own age eating together, studying together, and sleeping in the same dormitory or barracks. You will be randomly seated next to the same people week after week in classrooms for a whole term. How could anyone not make *some* friends in such a setting?

Being off on a new job in a new town is a different story, especially if you live alone. How then do you make friends?

Too many young people believe that the only place in a strange community that young people can meet each other is in a bar. It's not true and never has been.

Every year some of my students graduate and move from a college full of friendships to being all alone amid strangers in a graduate school or in a new job in a new town. I tell them to find a church right away.

I began my graduate work in Oregon. At church, on the first Sunday we were there, an older couple invited my wife and me and our two kids home for dinner. We later discovered that they were shirttail relatives of one of my uncles. That's not why they invited us. Neither of us knew we were related. They were just reaching out. Churches are full of people like that.

Sometimes, like it says in the Bible, we entertain "angels" without knowing it. Like the time I took a visitor home after church. My wife thought I was crazy to bring him home because we had so little to offer him. In those days we barely had enough to eat ourselves. But he graciously and thankfully ate the homemade bread and humble bowl of soup. Indeed, he seemed to enjoy simple food for a change. Several months later he arranged to get me my first writing job.

Church is one of the best places to look for friends, but it isn't the only place. Volunteer organizations and interest and hobby clubs on college campuses and in communities will put you together with others who have similar interests. Politics? Gardening? Health and fitness? There will be a group or a club near you. Find it and join. Friends are waiting.

Remember to include your need for friendship and community in your prayer requests. God knows your need and will answer it, often in wonderful and surprising ways.

Although we had been on the same college campus for almost a year without knowing it, I chanced to meet at a lake miles away from that campus the young woman who would become my wife. We almost missed each other. In a few weeks I would have graduated and we probably never would have met.

It wasn't chance. I believe God arranged that meeting. God somehow arranged for both of us to be at that lake on the same sunny afternoon. We have been blessed because of it.

God can also bless you with friendship and love. Not tomorrow, maybe, but sooner than you think.

Ask.

12

What about Alcohol and Drugs?

*T*alking about roommates and friends reminds me of Jon Appleside," Ann said.

"Johnny Appleseed?" Jenny lit up like a sparkler. "I haven't seen him since church camp two summers ago. He could really make a piano sing." She danced her fingers in the air as if she were playing a piano.

"And a guitar too," Ann said, strumming an air guitar.

"What's he doing?"

"He's in an alcohol treatment center."

"No. Jon? Really?" Jenny put both palms to her forehead in disbelief. "I thought he was at some music conservatory somewhere. Really? Jon? He was always so goody-goody."

"He hit some bad times," Ann said, shaking her head sadly from side to side. "If this were privileged information I wouldn't be telling you, but his mother told everyone about it at a teachers' meeting last week. I'm sure half the town knows by now."

"I didn't know," Jenny said sadly.

"I'm sorry to have been the one to tell you."

"How could it have happened?"

"I think his choice of friends had a lot to do with it. That's why I mentioned it. His mom blames that rock band he played with. They were drinking a lot, and occasionally mixing that with street drugs."

"Johnny Appleseed. I can hardly believe it."

"It can happen to anyone," Ann said. "That's the other side of making friends. Wild friends sometimes get you into trouble."

"Wild friends are sometimes exciting," Jenny said, with just a hint of baiting in her voice.

"Like Rick? Didn't you date Rick McCord a couple of years ago?" Jenny blushed. "I thought so. Is he what you mean by exciting?"

"I thought he was back then. Sure. He *was* exciting. At first anyway."

"Wild friends are like that. But as Christians we have to ask what those friendships will mean to our faith and to our moral choices."

"Now *you* sound like my mother!"

"Maybe, but it's true. The wild and the wonderful." When Ann said the word *wonderful* she pointed to Jenny. "When the wild and the wonderful get together, someone is either lifted up or dragged down. Which way was it with you and Rick?"

"We didn't go out after the second time. I was afraid he'd . . ." Jenny hesitated.

"Drag you down?"

"I guess that's it, now that you put a label on it."

"Alcohol and drugs and wild friends—and throw in sex for good measure—is the formula for getting dragged down. That's the way to lose your future—sometimes literally." Ann tapped her finger on her desk for emphasis. "Think of the kids in this town who have died in the last four or five years. How many of them have there been?"

"I don't know," Jenny shrugged. "Five or six maybe."

Ann leaned forward. "And how many died of what you would call 'natural causes'?"

Jenny scratched her head. "I can think of only one."

"How many died in drinking accidents and such?"

Jenny thought for many moments, then said, "Four."

"You see? The quickest way to lose your future. And sometimes I think that those who die are the lucky ones. Some kids are crippled for life—and in more ways than one. Some of them get into the chemical stuff and never get out. They'll never be right again."

"You mean brain-fried—like Andy Marks."

"Yeah," Ann said, "like Andy. I almost cry every time I see him. He was so bright and witty when I first met him."

"They ought to crucify drug dealers."

"They're trying. It's not working very well. But dealers aren't the biggest problem."

"They aren't?"

"No. It's the user. Waging war on drugs is like trying to ban chocolate. Too many people want

70

it. We have to attack on the demand side. Make kids—and adults—not ever want to *try* the stuff. Not even once."

"I haven't," Jenny said.

"You're in the minority. Even the casual use of something that seems harmless, like marijuana, makes so many kids drop out of everything." Ann moved to the edge of her chair and began to motion with her hands. "All illegal drugs are crime-related. If you follow even one marijuana cigarette back to its source, and then follow the money you pay for it to its destination, you'll uncover a mountain of corruption: bribery, extortion, prostitution, probably murder." Ann was talking fast and excitedly. This was one of her pet subjects. She was death on drugs.

"That's scary," Jenny said, her eyes wide.

"And alcohol, even though it's legal, has the same effect. Most young people aren't ready for it."

"Some people *never* are."

Jenny thought of her father. Ann thought of an uncle.

"Ever had any scary experiences with teen drinkers?" Ann asked.

Jenny nodded but didn't say anything.

"You don't have to tell me. Almost everyone has been at some risk. Age is so crucial. I was just now reminded of an uncle who used to drink quite a bit. He'd sometimes drive when he was somewhat impaired. He doesn't anymore, but he used to. I was with him once or twice, but it wasn't scary at all; he *knew* he was impaired and was even more careful."

"That's how they spot drunk drivers," Jenny said. "I read about it. The police watch for people who are driving too slowly."

"No one should ever drive impaired," Ann said, "but I'd take my uncle over most teenagers. Teenagers think they can guzzle that stuff all night and be as good as ever. Teenagers also think they're immortal. They can't even dream of dying themselves, much less hurting other people by what they do."

"I know," Jenny said sadly, remembering a couple of her friends.

"I remember three of us getting a ride home from a high school basketball game," Ann said, the anger already rising in her voice. "This guy was doing ninety on gravel roads. When we got out we vowed never to ride with him again. It was bad enough that we thought he just was a crazy driver. The next day we found out how much he had been drinking. That made it ten times worse. He could have killed all four of us—and other people too. I was furious."

"You were lucky."

"I guess we're all lucky to have survived our teen years."

"I haven't yet," Jenny smiled. "Two years to go."

"And that's just when you have to leave home and go off to a new place and find new friends and have no mother hovering over you—and *all that freedom*."

13

The
Safest Sex

*T*his could easily be the shortest chapter in this book, maybe in the history of book publishing: Chapter 13, "The Safest Sex." Paragraph 1, "Don't do it." End of chapter.

But you and I know it's not quite that easy.

My wife and daughter were with me as I was driving a twenty-four-foot-long U-Haul truck loaded with sets and display units for a convention in Detroit. Somewhere on the eastern edge of Chicago we missed an exit—but only by one hundred feet.

I pulled over on the shoulder and looked around. It was one of those spaghetti junctions with freeways crossing in several directions overhead. No one was behind me. Even though I knew it was against the law, I thought I could safely back up one hundred feet and drive down the ramp we had missed.

I put the truck into reverse. My back-up lights must have given me away because from one of those overhead ramps we heard what sounded like the thundering voice of God: "DON'T DO IT." It was a bullhorn on a police car.

Wouldn't life be much easier if God had a loud-speaker like that? Wouldn't our decisions be simplified if that warning voice—Don't do it!—were with us on picnics and at parties and in the back-seats of cars?

That's easier for me to write, of course, than for you to do (or not do). There are some good teen sexuality books around that can help. Look in a bookstore, ask your school librarian, or look in your church library. You may even run across another of my books, *It Takes Two* (Augsburg, 1987), a collection of stories about how some teens are handling these concerns.

They are *serious* concerns. I share my office lobby with the college health service. On walls and bulletin boards all around are posters and pamphlets that warn about AIDS, chlamydia, syphilis, gonorrhea, and abortion. Their under-lying message also is *don't do it*. But the very fact that they are hanging there reminds me every day that some students *do* do it. Actually, about fifty to sixty percent of college-age youth nationwide are or have been sexually active. The statistics for high schoolers are only slightly lower.

Back when I was young, the biggest fear of sex-ually active teens was pregnancy. You do it and you'll get pregnant—or you'll *get* somebody preg-nant. That fear can be minimized today, although statistics about unwanted pregnancies and abor-tions nationwide suggest that most teenagers who do it aren't being careful.

What we call "social diseases" seemed scarier back in my day. *Syphilis* and *gonorrhea* were frightening, unspoken words. No one had even heard of chlamydia or herpes back then, but they too were around. All those diseases were around—all except HPV (genital warts, imported from Korea by American soldiers) and AIDS. Your generation has all the old ones, *plus* these two new ones.

With all the publicity about AIDS, we aren't hearing so much about the other diseases. They are still out there. They are still unpleasant. Many of them can be controlled now with medications, but many of them still infect you for life and some of them still have the same horrible side effects: abnormal pregnancies, abnormal babies, cervical cancer, sterility. (Imagine having to tell your future husband or wife that you can never have a baby together because of some foolish choices you made when you were younger.)

The focus on AIDS is appropriate. It is a scary, growing epidemic. In North America AIDS is still prevalent mostly among drug users and homosexuals, but it is more and more being transmitted to unborn babies by infected mothers and to others through blood transfusions. AIDS is a threat to us all and is our number one health priority.

I read a headline yesterday that estimates that one in five hundred college students has the AIDS virus. By the time you read these words and get to college, that statistic will be even worse. It can only *get* worse.

The abortion issue gets more and more intense as well. The arguments for and against legalized abortion will make sense to different segments of the population, but for our purposes, let's just say that abortion is the world's worst method of birth control. That's how it's being used by too many young people. A young man and a young woman make a mistake, and a baby has to die for it.

AIDS, abortion, herpes, chlamydia. Scary. They are huge public health problems, but they will not be *your* problems if you *don't do it.*

I didn't do it. I'm neither bragging nor complaining. I just didn't, I never had sex with anyone before marriage and have been faithful to my wife and my vows ever since. That has been a wonderful and stable truth in our marriage. It is comforting too. We both know that neither of us has given or ever *can* give (the AIDS virus can be transmitted even ten years later) each other any of these diseases. And we haven't saddled our kids with any problems because of our youthful sexual decisions.

I had a former U.S. congressman speak to my class last term. He listed the two most important things he found in college: (1) becoming renewed in his Christian faith, and (2) finding his wife. He talked about how important being sexually faithful had been for them, especially amid the temptations in Washington, D.C.

Keeping marriage vows is not your concern yet, but it will be someday. God doesn't want you to break vows then; God doesn't want you to fornicate now. Not doing it now will make it easier then, and that is part of what I think is the biggest reason not to do it today: bonding.

The Bible tells us that sexual intercourse is designed by God to be the most profound and wonderful bonding of two human beings. That bonding is designed to show faithful love and can result in the birth of children into a home with two loving, caring, nurturing parents. It doesn't always work out that way, but that's the way God designed sexuality.

Recreational sex is therefore a false bonding. A couple's whole future is supposed to be in that act. On a subconscious level, a human being believes sex to be part of a psychological and spiritual bonding that looks far ahead toward a life together, the raising of children, and building a home.

Recreational sex destroys that—not only for now, but for the future when real bonding with real sexual communion should happen.

Don't take that risk. If you are taking it, quit. If you aren't sure whether your present sexual relationship is recreational or bonding, try this: Go cold turkey for three months and see if you are still friends.

Going backwards in a physical relationship is difficult. That's why it's too bad so many young people are getting too physical too soon. It can be done, though. Ask for help. Go to your pastor or your youth director (someone like Ann in our dialogues), a school counselor, a teacher, or some other Christian adult that you respect and trust. Tell that person what's going on in your sex life and what you want to do about it.

Remember that Jesus is also the Lord of starting over. The forgiving love of Jesus can wash and renew anyone, any time, any place. In John 7:53— 8:11 Jesus said to the adulterous woman, "Go now and leave your life of sin." It's a good story. Read it. Some think that none of the teachers of the law and Pharisees dared throw the first stone because Jesus was scribbling in the sand the names of their old girlfriends. Some also think that the woman was Mary, the sister of Martha and Lazarus.

Whoever she was, it's a wonderful story of starting over. A friend of ours once joked, "I got my virginity back when I went to college." It may not be quite that easy, but leaving your hometown and school and friends and family for college or work or the military service is a good time to make some important changes in your life. One of those changes could be resolving to go back on the inactive list.

14

Marriage: When or Whether

So how are you and Scott doing?" Ann asked during a lull in their discussion of the other topics.

"Depends on what day you ask," Jenny said with a wry smile.

"What does that mean?"

"Sometimes I see him in my future, and sometimes I don't."

"Does he think that way too?"

"I don't know. Maybe when he's being honest."

"Isn't he honest?"

"He's such an *idealist*." Jenny said, shaking her head. "He thinks marriage will solve all his problems."

"You mean at home?" Ann asked, knowing almost as much as Jenny did about Scott's troubled family.

"Mostly that."

"Marriage," Ann said, "doesn't solve anything. It usually creates even *more* problems. You take all the old baggage with you and then add to that all the adjustment and compromise of early marriage. Just ask your mom."

Jenny looked down at her hands and didn't say anything. Her parents had divorced ten years earlier. "I'm sorry," Ann said after a few moments. "I didn't say that to hurt you."

"I know. It's just that a dozen times a day I wish for a father. I wouldn't even mind the divorce part so much if my father would just father me sometimes."

"He probably can't," Ann said, trying to sound as sympathetic as she felt.

"Why did he get married then?" Jenny began to cry softly, putting her elbows on her knees and pressing the heels of her hands into her eye sockets as if trying to keep the tears from coming.

"Who can say why people get married," Ann said, knowing she was going to have to do a monologue for a minute or two while Jenny calmed down. Ann rolled her office chair around the corner of the desk until she was next to Jenny. As Ann continued to speak, she massaged Jenny's shoulders and back gently.

"Marriage is so strange," Ann went on. "Everyone expects so much from it. And it doesn't help that it starts out with such a huge splash: a big wedding celebration, tons of gifts, and then maybe a honeymoon trip. Coming down off of a high like that is tough. A couple of older women I know never *have* come down. That's still the highlight of their lives." Jenny nodded and tried inhaling in three short breaths.

"I was reading a book on marriage just last week," Ann went on. "The author said that almost all couples start with a dangerous overdose of self-confidence. I expect your parents did."

Ann paused then, not wanting to bring up that painful subject again. She decided to try what often worked when she was talking to her youth group and had started to lose their attention: confession. "I almost got married once," Ann whispered.

It worked. Jenny broke out of her self-pity. She sat up and took the tissue Ann handed her. "Really?" she said, and then blew her nose with a sharp snort.

"Uh huh. His name was Tom. We were actually in the print shop looking at samples of wedding invitations when my doubts got serious enough to notice."

"You were that close?" Jenny said, wide-eyed and stifling an involuntary sob.

"That close. I guess we would have made it work. I know we would have tried awfully hard."

"What happened?" Jenny noticed a sad look in Ann's eyes.

"Like a prophetess, I guess, I envisioned the future. Tom was training to be a businessman like his father. His father ran a big employment agency just outside of Cleveland."

"What was wrong with that?"

"I don't know. I guess standing there in that print shop with the smell of ink so insistent made me remember my dream of writing a book about Russia. I tried to see into the future at that moment. I couldn't picture Tom's house with a word processor and me in front of it. The image just wasn't there." Ann took a deep breath.

"All I could see," she went on, "was *Tom's* future. His *whole* future: He would take over his father's business when his father retired to Florida. We'd have a house on the hill. Our three beautiful kids would go to the best private colleges. Twenty years of homemaking and volunteer work later, one of them would take over the business. Then *we'd* retire in Florida too." Ann's smile became broader as she narrated.

"That doesn't sound so terrible." Jenny smiled with her.

"It sounded awful to me. The American nightmare. I wanted some surprises in my life."

"Will you ever try again? Marriage I mean?"

"I don't know. I'm thirty-three next month. Think of it, thirty-three. That's one-third of one hundred."

"But it's only one-sixth of two hundred." Jenny laughed; Ann rolled her eyes.

"One poll I read about said unmarried women are the happiest people."

"I wonder if my mom would agree with that." Jenny said.

"But I believe in marriage," Ann said forcefully. "Stable marriages are at the very center of the kind of society I want to live in. Marriages like my parents have."

"It's good, is it?"

"One of the best I know. They're almost sixty now, but they're in love like high school kids."

"I wish it could always be that way. How can people stay like that?" Jenny asked, slumping so that her chin rested in her palm.

"I can only speak for my parents."

"How did they do it, then?"

"I think they were both fairly careful and se-
lective when they chose each other. I think it
helped that they were of similar social, educa-
tional, and religious backgrounds. And when they
went for it, they committed themselves to each
other absolutely, before God."

"I hope I can do that," Jenny said, envisioning
herself standing at an altar.

"You will. Just remember that you are going to
have to work at it. I remember my mom used to
chase my dad around the house when he was
upset. She'd follow him around like a lioness
stalking prey. She'd do the twenty questions thing
on him until he finally started to talk. Then they'd
talk it out together. She was wonderful about that."

"Why do you say *was?*"

"They communicate so much better now that
they hardly ever fight."

"Old couples should teach young couples
about that."

"I don't know if they could," Ann said. "Maybe
that sort of thing has to be experienced. There
are classes and courses in churches and in communities to help couples work those things out."

"But that's after they have chosen each other
for sure," Jenny said. "Why isn't there a group
Scott and I could go to, one that would help us
decide whether we should get married *at all?*"

"Only God knows that."

"But how can *we* be sure?"

"Give it a little time. Don't make any long-term
commitments right now. You'll be in college in a
year or two."

"So?"

"So only a few hometown romances survive the separation and the new acquaintances of college."

"I guess that's what scares Scott when I start to talk about college. That means a long wait, doesn't it?"

"It won't *seem* long. If you choose right, you can expect to be married forty or fifty years or more. Take some time now, on the front end, to make sure you'll still be together on the far end."

"It seems harder these days."

"It's always been hard. The only difference is that today's society doesn't force couples into marriage. It doesn't force them to stay in a destructive marriage either."

"Getting out of it seems too easy somehow."

"That's part of what makes so many young marriages fail, I think." Ann stood up and paced the office floor, slapping a finger in her palm for each point she made. "They have high expectations but too much independence and selfishness. That creates a high probability of serious difficulties. Add to that the low tolerance most young people have for struggle and compromise, and their not having enough good role models, and you have our modern marriage mess."

"Is there any hope?" Jenny asked.

"I haven't given up on marriage," Ann said. "Not for me and not for society either. I've seen some wonderful marriages right here in our church, young people and old. They put everything they've got into it—including a lot of faith and prayer."

"I hope I'll be able to do that."

"Don't worry about it yet. Just keep your eye out for the right person and wait for the right time. If it's Scott, it'll be Scott. Just be sure to hold out for that complete commitment. Don't do it half way."

"What do you mean, 'half way'?"

"Living together. Maybe circumstances keep some people from marrying when they should. But I'd rather just get married sooner and then struggle *together* to finish school or get that job or whatever else it is that makes people live together rather than get married."

"But what if they try being together like that and discover that it doesn't work out?" Jenny asked. "Isn't it easier then *not* to be married?"

"Being together is never easy. Too often living together involves only half a commitment. People start out thinking, 'Well, if this doesn't work out, at least we're not married.' That partial commitment dooms the relationship before it even gets started. Who knows how many couples who failed at living together could have made a real marriage work. How many would have settled into a real marriage and knocked heads until they *learned* how to be together if they were constantly being nudged by the full commitment of their vows. Wouldn't most of them work harder at it? Wouldn't you?"

Jenny just nodded.

15

What Kind of Job Should I Get?

*B*ecause I spend so much time writing, I only teach part-time. Pay for part-time teachers isn't that good, but I tell myself I don't do it for the money. My work is play. I have fun writing and enjoy teaching so much that if someone asked me, I might even do it for nothing.

Some of my writing is for free: children's plays, poems for birthdays and anniversaries and retirements, devotions, wedding and funeral sermons for relatives and friends. It needs to be done. I am glad to do it.

The work we start out doing when we are young isn't often our life's work, but we learn from it— and it gets us on *toward* our life's work.

Keep on searching until you find work you love. Sometimes that search takes years, and sometimes you have a few false starts (that whole process is discussed in several places throughout this book). But keep searching until you find joy in your work.

Some of you young people are already making the mistake of following someone else's dream. Maybe it's your parents' dream that you become a doctor or lawyer, or your grandma's dream that you be a pastor or missionary, or maybe some dream of your own that drives you to be *better* than, or do something more *important* than, your brothers or sisters. Maybe you want to prove something to your peers or your old girlfriend, or to your hometown—to show them and everyone else that you *are* going to amount to something.

Some students try to excel academically to compensate for some other ability they think they lack. It's almost like their minds whisper: *You can't be popular, you can't make any of the athletic teams or musical groups in school, you can't be class president or a cheerleader, but no one can stop you from being the best student in your class.*

So that's what the person becomes. The study marathon begins. Does it bring happiness? Probably not. It will have its satisfactions and will open a lot of doors to good colleges and universities, good graduate programs, and good jobs, but there may not be much joy.

Some people never find much joy in their work, but compensate by finding happiness in their hobbies. That's OK, too. People don't often leap for joy over the jobs they have to do day in and day out, but they keep doing those jobs to pay the bills. They get their satisfaction *after* work. When the bills are all paid, they have enough left over to buy tools and lumber for their amateur carpentry projects, or yarn and needles and patterns for their knitting, or flower bulbs for the garden, or beat-up antique furniture to refinish.

Sometimes the hobby becomes the vocation. Let's say a young married man is trained in something specialized like city planning, but can't find work in the college town in which his wife teaches. So he stays home and cares for their baby.

He discovers that he enjoys it. After a while he offers to care for the children of a couple of friends as well. He finds that caring for three kids isn't that much more work than caring for one.

Three years later he has gone into partnership with another husband. The two of them are earning good second incomes running Dad's Day-care Center—and they love it.

Dan, a physics professor, over a period of years turned his hobby, fly fishing, into his work. He began tying flies (little bits of feather and hair and yarn and thread that, to trout, look like delicious insects) and selling them. Dan's fly shop in Livingston, Montana, now has a national and international reputation. He employs forty to fifty full-time professional fly-tyers who create three to four hundred different types of flies.

It's not that easy, though, for most of us. Then where do we turn? A lot of times when we are confused someone will ask, "Well, what does the Bible say?"

When it comes to work, the Bible isn't always easy to understand. Some passages and parables say that faithfulness and hard work are bound to pay off. Elsewhere, we are advised to do our best, then sit back and be content like the birds and the flowers. These are the words of Jesus: "Do not worry about your life, what you will eat or drink; or about your body, what you will wear" (Matt. 6:25). Compare that with these words from St.

Paul: "If a man will not work, he shall not eat" (2 Thess. 3:10).

There's probably a happy middle ground for most people who work—for students, for fast-food workers and pizza deliverers, and for executives in major corporations. Maybe you have heard it said, "All work and no play makes Jack a dull boy." (Or Jill a dull girl.) All play and no work is probably worse. At least the workaholic earns his or her own keep.

Workaholism is one of the recurring themes in essays written by my first-year college students. It usually results in the loss of fathers. It's not that the fathers have died or the parents have been divorced, or even that the father is an alcoholic (although that has much the same effect).

The problem is the father's work habits. He works all the time. It's often daughters who write these essays. Somewhere along about fourth or fifth grade the father starts to disappear, and by high school he's gone altogether. He leaves early, comes home late, travels a lot, works weekends, and spends his spare time with associates and clients. He never has time to attend the kids' games, recitals, or concerts.

The women's movement and new career opportunities for women have made overwork a problem for many women as well. More and more we will see the "disappearing mother" act in our modern society. Don't get caught up in it, either you young men or you young women.

Work is not meant to consume your life; work is not meant to be the sole aim of your life. Work is meant to serve God and fellow human beings.

Some working people need constantly to be reminded that the nearest fellow human beings are *in their own families.*

What would it profit someone, even in the most dedicated sort of service work (doctor, nurse, counselor, pastor, missionary) to help the whole world and lose his or her own daughter or son?

Start when you are young to get a good fix on the place of the family in your work life. Ask people you admire how they balance work and play and hobbies and home life. Talk with your parents about it. Survey your own value system and see just what you think is worth working for now, and what you think you will want to work for and achieve in the years to come.

16

Narrowing Job Choices

Job hunting depends a lot on attitude. If you start out thinking there's nothing available, nothing will be. If you start out thinking you couldn't possibly be qualified for anything, you won't be. If you start out thinking you won't like any sort of work that *might* be available or that *you* could get, you won't.

You have to start with optimism, an attitude that sees job opportunities everywhere, that whispers in your ear that you can do almost anything, and that puts dreams in your mind and creates job opportunities, even when there don't seem to be any.

Our daughter Shelley was that way. Sometime in early spring before her high school summers, she'd carefully search *The Yellow Pages* reminding herself of the businesses in town, then walk downtown and have a look. She'd come home, make a list of a half-dozen places she'd like to work, then walk into store after store and say, "I'm looking for a job and I'd like to work here." Getting a job never took her more than two days.

She's still doing that. This year she picked out the two publishing houses she really wanted to work for, put together a strong resume, and applied at both. Her first job offer came two days after her resume was received. Eventually, the other company also offered her a job.

Not all job searches have to be so pointed or so profound. But if you are looking for a job, maybe that method also would work for you. Think of the businesses in your area. How could they use a person of your age and with your abilities and experience? Think hard about it. Maybe you'll come up with an idea that business has never thought of or tried—but something that might work. Then walk in confidently and suggest your idea—and yourself as the logical person to try it.

The farther along you get in life, the fussier you will probably get about jobs. Corporate employment agencies tell their clients they may have to job hunt one month for every $10,000 in salary they expect to get. For some that means a year or more.

At your age, though, the sort of job you get may not be that deadly serious. It doesn't even pay to get too fussy. You can, however, ask some broad and general questions about yourself that will not only make your search easier, but may actually keep you out of some employment disasters.

First, there are people questions:

1. Do you like being with people?
2. Could you stay calm with an upset, dissatisfied customer?

3. Would you do better dealing with people on the telephone rather than face to face?
4. Can you take orders from a boss or supervisor?
5. Could you work for a picky, pushy manager?
6. Could you keep working all by yourself, all day, in the back room of a busy store?

Maybe you would rather work for yourself than someone else. If so, what skills and experience do you have that others would pay for?

Pete, a former student, wrote about how he started mowing large suburban lawns in his neighborhood when he was in junior high. He worked hard to satisfy his customers and over several summers one lawn led to another. In the summer of his junior year he invested $5000 in commercial lawn-mowing equipment. It was a big risk, but he paid for his equipment the first summer and continues to help pay for his college education by mowing lawns.

Marla did the same thing with baby-sitting. She loved doing it and was so good at it that soon there were more jobs than she had time for. She began referring callers to her younger sister, then to several friends she trusted. Soon she was managing a baby-sitting service.

My oldest son Scott began roofing porches and garages for neighbors and friends when he was fifteen. He is twice that old now, has gone to college and will go to graduate school, supporting himself and his family by roofing and painting houses.

Neither Pete nor Marla nor Scott will probably run a lawn-mowing or baby-sitting service or roof houses for many more years, but they will all have learned a lot about business and work and people and themselves while being their own bosses.

After answering the people questions, you should maybe ask some environmental questions, not questions about acid rain and water pollution, but questions like these:

1. Where do you like to work?
2. Would you rather plant trees in the woods or sell hamburgers on Main Street?
3. At camp, would you rather be a lifeguard and sit in the sun all day, or sit inside and teach crafts?
4. Would you rather work on a road crew or organize sets of prints in a photo-finishing shop?
5. Would a job far from home make you unreasonably homesick for your family or your sweetheart?

Job and vocational inventories ask you those kinds of questions, and you would do well to ask yourself those questions. If you have trouble with the answers, run the questions by your parents and friends. Start by asking, "What kind of job do you think I'd like?"

After people and environment questions, you may want to answer some questions also about the level of brain and brawn you'd need to invest in certain kinds of work. Like:

1. Would you rather spend your working time thinking or doing?
2. What do you want to shove around, cement blocks or sheets of paper?
3. What do you want to help build, apartment houses or relationships?

Some work is physical, like construction, delivery, and maintenance. Some is more intellectual like bookkeeping, running a checkout, being a library assistant, or reading for the blind. What would you rather do? These are important distinctions.

After all these practical questions are faced, what if where you live, there is nothing available but fast-food jobs?

Then take a fast-food job.

It's better to be working than to be sitting at home pretending to be fussy.

Every job is a learning experience and every job is worth doing well. Even work that seems miserable and disastrous while you are doing it will often teach you valuable lessons, especially when you look back at it years later. Your disasters may even seem funny in retrospect.

I sometimes have my first-year college students write essays about work. Some of the essays are deadly serious, but some of them look back on work experiences with a real sense of humor.

One young man started a fire in the french-fry kettle at McDonalds. One young woman forgot to turn off a faucet and caused a flood. Waiters and waitresses write about dropping trays full of food and beverages, of drenching customers in water, soup, or spaghetti.

A pizza delivery person wrote about putting himself out of business by driving too fast on slippery streets and totalling his car. A construction worker left a parked truck out of gear and it rolled into the river. A young woman operating a tractor loader for the first time dropped a log, just missing her boss, but completely crushing a new power lawnmower.

And they all had stories about coworkers—wonderful, helpful, zany, unusual, and memorable coworkers—who gave them new views of the variety and splendor and eccentricity of God's human species.

Youthful work lessons are wonderful and important. It's getting close to a half century since I got my first job, but I still vividly remember some of those early work scenes. Build your own memories, and build your future as a worker—starting with the many interesting, intriguing, and challenging part-time jobs you will hold over the years. Be glad for your associations with interesting, intriguing, and challenging coworkers.

God bless you as you find your way from job to job, from challenge to challenge, from opportunity to opportunity. God help you finally to find vocation, a calling, a sense that this is where it has all been leading.

When you have finally found your vocation, you will have a wonderful awareness of God's guidance and grace in your life, and that will lead to a profound sense of satisfaction and peace.

God grant you that peace.

17

Job Search

So if you don't marry Scott," Ann asked as she checked her watch against the church chimes overhead, "and if you don't start college this year, what are you going to do?"

"I'll work I guess," Jenny replied, staring at Ann's watch as if it were ticking her very life away.

"What kind of job?"

"I don't know. That's my next problem."

"I myself haven't had much experience with job hunts. I told you how my first youth work job just happened."

"I wish something would just happen to me," Jenny said.

"Sometimes it does. Sometimes you just hear about a job. But more likely those 'just happens' appear because you've used the network."

"What's a network?"

"Your contacts. That's the first place to start a job search. Like with me. You come to my office and say, 'Ann, I think I'll work a year or two before college,' and so on. Let's try it. Let's do a little network role play."

"Will it be stupid?" Jenny asked sheepishly. "The last role play we did in youth group was kind of stupid."

"We won't let it be stupid this time. Come on. Pretend you just came into my office. Say to me what I just said to you."

"Well, OK. Here goes: Ann, I think I'll work for a year or two before I go to college."

"Sounds like you're beginning to work out a plan for your life," Ann said in a voice as deep as the voice of God. "What sort of work will you look for?" She strolled around the office with her hands behind her back like a factory owner in an old movie.

"You said it wasn't going to be corny!" Jenny said in an exasperated voice.

"I was kidding. Keep on."

"OK. I thought you could maybe help me find a job. I thought maybe you'd have ideas and con-tacts."

"Good, good," Ann said. "You're getting the idea."

"Well, do you?" Jenny stared, her eyes wide.

"Do I what?"

"Do you have any ideas or contacts—I mean, for real? I think I really *should* work for a while. I guess if I were going to develop a *network* as you call it," Jenny said, "you'd be one of the first people I'd ask."

"I'm pleased to hear that." Ann smiled.

"Well, do you have any ideas?"

"One of the things I'd do is give you some other names. I'd suggest that you go to the pastor, for instance, then to Mr. Rodriguez. He's the president of our congregation. Do you know him?"

"No."

"It wouldn't matter. You'd just say that I sent you, or the pastor sent you. He's not only president of our congregation, he's been president of the chamber of commerce for as long as I've worked here."

"He'd know a lot of business people then," Jenny said, nodding.

"He'd know most of them. Now then. Do *you* know anyone in town you could work for?"

"Let's see. My mom went to high school with Mr. Thomas."

"Who's that?"

"Fairchild Foods."

"Oh yeah. That should be a good contact. Would you like to work as a checkout person? Or behind the deli counter?"

"I guess I wouldn't mind, at least for a year or so."

"Anyone else?"

"Mrs. Pei lives across the street. She and my mom are friends. She and her husband run the Mandarin Garden Restaurant."

"Really? Oh how I love their mandarin pork!"

"They use college kids for waiting tables. I've always thought I was too young. But this summer I'll be old enough, won't I?"

"Sure you will. Are your mom and Mrs. Pei *good* friends?"

"Sure. I know she'd give me a try."

"Would you like that?" Ann asked.

"I think I would. I'd meet a lot of people, and the tips would be good."

"The tips would only be good if you were a good waitress. Have you thought of how you'd prepare for a waitressing job?"

"Prepare? How could you?" Jenny asked, wide-eyed.

"There are many things to learn. Books to read. Books on waitressing and Chinese food. Lots of questions to ask, too. Serving with grace and elegance is a lot more than just interrupting someone's conversation every five minutes to chant, 'Everything OH-KAAAY?' "

Jenny laughed, remembering waitresses who did that all the time. "That's like some clerk saying 'Have a good day,' when your mountain bike was stolen in the morning and your favorite grandma's funeral was that afternoon."

"You see what I mean about networking, though. I guess that half the jobs are filled by networking. Someone asks someone who knows someone who tells someone. A lot of the best promotions are internal, too."

"Meaning what?"

"Meaning from inside. Let's say that you went to Mr. Thomas at the Fairchild Food Market. Let's say you decided you'd like to work in the deli. But let's say what he *really* needed was an assistant manager."

"I'd take that," Jenny laughed.

"I'm *sure* you would. But he'd probably hire someone *qualified*, someone he knew. So he'd promote the produce manager to assistant manager, he'd promote the head stocker to be produce manager, and then promote one of the assistant stockers to head stocker. By now what he really needs is a new stockperson."

"So that's the job he'd offer me?"

"Right. And the only qualifications would be the ability to work fairly steadily, to walk several miles a day, to notice and remember what's needed on shelves, and to lift fifty-pound boxes. Can you lift fifty pounds?"

"Sure."

"You see who often gets the better jobs?"

"The people who started from the bottom. So the assistant manager started as a stockperson?"

"Of course she did. And because she's been finishing her college degree as she's worked, she's going to move into corporate management in a few years. She's on her way."

"I wish it was as easy in real life as it is in your imagination."

"It's never really easy," Ann said. "Some people have jobs dumped in their laps, but once you get a job, you have to do it. No job is that easy to do. People who make their own opportunities, who network, who study the job market, and keep their options open, are usually the same ones who work hard from day one and move up on the job."

"A lot of times they move from one business to another too. That's how they get their promotions. Let's say that this same woman feels that she will never get into top management in her store because the owner's son is coming along right behind her. She knows that when the time comes for the manager to retire, he'll promote his son right past her. So she makes some discreet visits to other stores in the area. She's looking for a place with a future. She has the experience and the ability; all she needs is an opening."

"It sounds like finding jobs and getting promotions are do-it-yourself operations," Jenny said.

"We can't sit here in a church and fully believe that," Ann said. "It doesn't really say in the Bible that God helps those who help themselves, but God empowers us to do what has to be done. That's what we ought to pray for—not so much for miracles as for strength and insight to get things done for ourselves, or sometimes just to accept things as they are."

"I guess you're right."

"You'll see. You'll start your job search with networking. You'll study the 'help-wanted' ads, and you may have a session or two with an employment counselor, or maybe register with a temporary help company to get yourself started. You'll figure out how to get a job."

"I wish I had as much confidence in me as you have," Jenny said.

"You should have. You're smart, you have your good health, and you're ambitious. Should someone like you have trouble finding a job?"

A broad smile spread across Jenny's face. She jabbed her fist in the air and said, "No! Never!"

18

What If My Plan Isn't God's Plan?

Jenny has been getting good advice from Ann, but it's all hypothetical, it's all based on ifs and thens. *If* I do this, *then* this might happen. Few people *my* age, when they were *your* age, knew exactly where they would be and what they would be doing for the next twenty-five or thirty years.

I sure didn't. We are quite settled down now. We are back in the Midwest where we started out and where our roots are. But we're back after an odyssey of work and education that took us from Minnesota to Oregon to Texas then back to Oregon then back to Texas then to Canada and finally back home to Minnesota.

I sometimes wonder whether I missed some message from God somewhere along the way. If we're right back where we started from years ago, wouldn't it have been better for me and easier on my family if we had just stayed right here in the first place? Should I have gotten some sort of message about that?

Could it be that my wanderlust was just a part of some grand plan of God for our family? Moving was frustrating and expensive, and took massive blocks of time. God understands all that, of course, and often lets us do what seems right at the time, using our decisions, even our misguided ones, to herd us toward some sort of goal or goals that only God could understand beforehand.

How did God get our family to keep moving? Not by lofty dreams and visions like you read about in the Bible. Quite the opposite, in fact. God let me, or maybe I let myself, become dissatisfied sometimes, peevish sometimes, frustrated, feeling unwanted or unappreciated. I had to confront environments, climates, problems, and situations that after a while I wanted more to move away from than to live with. My poor family was also saddled with those decisions.

Perhaps things have happened also in your family that have made you feel pushed around. Maybe at moments when you are sitting there thinking about who you are and where you are and what you're doing, your whole life may seem like some gigantic goof-up—like some joke God is playing on you.

Those thoughts are bound to come when you can't find a job, have just quit one (or gotten fired), were not accepted by your three first-choice colleges, recently broke up with your beloved or broke an engagement (or had either happen to you), quit school (or flunked out), or didn't get the job or the promotion or the scholarship or something that you really wanted and had been hoping, and yes, praying for.

Think about prayer for a moment. If you see God as a sort of super parent figure, and if you see Jesus as a wonderfully wise big brother, then prayer will seem to you a lot like sharing things with someone more experienced and with a larger view of the future than you.

If you take time to remember who hears your prayer, then it ought to seem like discussing a possibility with someone who can see all likely consequences. Being all-knowing is wonderful for God, but it certainly would be scary for us. None of us would even dare get out of bed in the morning if we knew exactly what was going to happen to us and everyone around us all day long.

So we live on faith and hope—and we pray. Because God can see beforehand the consequences of our decisions and actions, sometimes God's wise and gracious answer to things we ask for is a big and definite NO.

God doesn't always say no. Some of our prayers are answered exactly as we expect. Other good things happen that we never prayed about. Bad things happen too, and sometimes because too many of our decisions aren't well connected to God. We do some things without much faith or thought or prayer. Some of them work out and some don't. Some are absolute disasters. But God is with us even then, comforting us, trying always to guide and direct us through the Holy Spirit.

Though there seem to be many twists and turns and disappointments and heartbreaks in our lives, we should never start to think that God is bashing us around or teasing us. God doesn't do that. God doesn't make bad things happen to people either. Satan, the evil one, does.

Sometimes things seem to happen just by accident. Someone is always getting on the wrong side of one of the laws of nature. People fall and sink and break. Machines fail. Lightning strikes. Hurricanes and floods happen. We don't look where we're going or are in the wrong place at the wrong time. The foolishness of others often hurts the innocent. People suffer terribly and sometimes die. The world is not always a happy place.

But being faithful to God helps us make some use of even the worst things that happen. Your path has already been difficult at times, and probably at times seemed unfair. That will continue all your life. You won't get to do what you want or go where you want a lot of the time, but maybe some of the roadblocks and detours that you confront are God's way of giving you experience and wisdom and patience. God may also be protecting you. By saying no, God may be directing you toward something better.

Some of our roadblocks and messes come from pulling away from God. When people shut God out of their lives for large blocks of time—or forever—they are soon making more and more Godless choices and getting themselves into more trouble than they ever dreamed possible. When we begin to think we can live our lives without our God and our Savior, times will soon get rocky, scary, and even dangerous.

So we pray and read the Scriptures and talk to people who want to help us as Jenny did with Ann. We give ourselves to God and let God move us into the future.

This next observation won't sound too wonderful to you, especially after you read this far, but here it is: *Most of us can see God's pathways better when we're looking backwards.*

When we have at least lived enough years to see where we've been, our lives sometimes begin to make sense. I know that isn't much comfort. You'd probably like to have a lifetime roadmap, highlighted by God in blaze orange, with warning notes and suggestions written all over it, and with a life's work—and maybe a life's partner—all picked out and planned out.

Only a rare few are blessed and privileged to know even a little of God's plan for their lives beforehand. Few seventh graders can say: "God wants me to be a teacher or a missionary or a pastor or a youth worker—and to marry Gary Baxter when I'm twenty-three." Those who are graduating from high school may think they know, but most of them will change their minds and their career choices many times in the years to come. It's more likely, as with Ann in our dialogues, that we will stumble onto God's pathway later in life.

The teen years, and the twenties too, are times of high idealism and lofty goals. You probably feel that deeply right now. You want desperately to do something useful and wonderful with your life.

And you will.

But maybe not in exactly the way you are dreaming of now.

As we grow older, we see more clearly how God has, can, and will use our abilities and talents and opportunities. After a while we become satisfied with that. We finally become somewhat content, at peace, with who we are and what we do.

But that time is a long way off for you—and you can thank God for that. Your dreams and your hopes and your ideals are some of the ways God blasts you off into your early-year's activities. How else could God motivate you to keep going through the pain and pleasure, frustration and satisfaction, failure and success that is ahead of you?

Hold on to your dreams as long as you can. Test them. Weigh them. Try your best, with God's help, to achieve them. Some of your dreams will come true. Some things will happen in your life that are more wonderful than your dreams.

Some unpleasant things will happen too. There will be disappointments. Some of the dreams you now cherish will die or be pushed aside. Some dreams, like the hope of heaven for instance, will be there all your life to keep you reaching out ahead of yourself, to keep you moving onward, and to keep the Spirit busy sanctifying you, making you day by day more holy and more useful.

Going after some of my impossible dreams has at least allowed me to be a part-time writer and teacher and preacher. I'm not the best at any of them, but by God's grace and goodness I get to do some of all three.

Some of *your* dreams will come true as well. Maybe not at the time you envision or in the ways you envision. But they will come true. Some of them. Trust me about that.

Rather, trust God about that.

19

Looking Forward

*T*his book is ending just when your life is about to blossom. The life ahead of you will be full of all sorts of exciting and challenging and mystifying and frightening and wonderful and satisfying (I could go on adding adjectives for two pages) experiences.

You are blessed to have so much of your life left to live. Although I'm glad for you, I don't really envy you because I've already been through it once. I don't wish I had my life to live over. I hope you never do either.

Even though I don't want to live my youth over, I really do enjoy watching young people like you live yours. I enjoy sharing your thrills and fears as you face an interesting and challenging future. That's probably why I enjoy teaching so much. I work with young men and women of great potential who are making important life choices every day.

As you live through the next few years, I hope you will stay close to God, both in prayer and the Scriptures, and in the church. Sinful and misguided and cliquish as the church may sometimes seem, *it is God's family on earth*. The church is also where others will pray with you and for you, and where you can go to find God's Word believed and taught and preached.

I mentioned earlier how, for us, finding a church has always come first in a new town or a new situation. Through our church connections we have kept our worship life uninterrupted and have made many friends. Our church connections have often been more satisfying and long-lasting than the work connections. The church has been an important part of our past and is important to our future as well.

◆

Life should be lived day by day, minute by minute—not sitting around in semiboredom waiting for something "important" to happen, like weekends or big dates or birthdays or holidays. Don't refuse to live life between "happenings." Don't wish your life away by looking too far ahead, by holding your breath, by withholding eager and full participation in life until you are older or farther along. Live your life now. Let it unfold.

As it unfolds, don't be too easily disappointed or turned off. Things don't usually happen as fast as we want. Sometimes we have to spend more time learning and experiencing, "paying our dues," before we get to do what we have always dreamed of doing—or to do even *part* of what we have dreamed of doing.

To achieve your dream, you may have to go to school for a long time. You may have to work your way up from the bottom, or work at a *related* job before you can get the job you really want. You may have to invest a lot of time learning, or doing volunteer work, or doing your thing free before you have earned the right to get paid for it. (For example, a junior counselor at a camp moves up to paid staff and finally to camp director.)

Remember too that your apprentice years are also years of your life. The fourteen years I spent in college, seminary, and graduate school were not lived in a vacuum. I didn't and couldn't set my life aside while I got my academic degrees. We had children to raise. We had next-door neighbors. We had friends and family.

So many important things happened in those years. In my college years I taught third grade Sunday school. I am now teaching the children of those children. I also met my wife in college. In later school years we had our children and we saw other parts of the country and we made still other friends. We bought our first little house. We fished and camped and beachcombed. We had a wonderful time.

Sure, I was busy in school and, sure, we were poor. But we were living important years of our lives as husband, wife, workers, students, children, and as a family. During all those years we were God's children, walking on the paths that led us to where we are now. We enjoyed it—most of the time. It was God's joy.

You too should have God's joy. God wants you to have it. If you take away no other truth from this book than this one, take it: GOD WANTS YOU TO HAVE JOY, *NOW*.

Don't postpone living now in order to achieve some future reward or goal. Work hard at it, sure. Give your goals and your dreams your very best. But do not quit living meanwhile.

I've seen too much of that. I've seen too many students who bury themselves in some isolated corner of the college library and come out four years later as 4.0, straight A misfits. Or young husbands and fathers who are so driven to succeed that they cease being husbands and fathers, or young women who are so career oriented that they ignore or refuse love and romance.

Don't do that. No college or university or corporation or career or job can ever own you, or have any right to rob you of your joy.

God owns you.

And God wants you to have joy.

Now.

God bless you on your way. God bless you along your exciting, satisfying, and joyful journey.

I hope when you are my age you will be able to look back and see that God's hand has been guiding you all along. Your faith, your love, and your continuing close connection to God the Father, Son, and Holy Spirit can help that happen.